LIVE WIDE

ELIZABETH DISTEL GRADY

Advance Praise

Written for the NYT's Book Review, By CC Laurence

The narrator in Elizabeth Mary Catherine's literary debut, "Live W I D E," is a restless, introspective woman with an appetite for life. Of Midwestern values, Elizabeth has always been tenacious and the consummate perfectionist. EMC becomes an up and coming media director in the advertising industry in Chicago, only to have her career interrupted by cancer in August 1998. And not just a garden variety, but a "Dragon." Elizabeth's odds of being diagnosed with a rare and aggressive HER2+ inflammatory breast cancer in her 30's, were one in a million. Her odds of beating it were just as slim. In spite of this frightening prognosis, she approaches "Project Beth" with strategic finesse, fierce competitiveness and a campaign slogan. "I am worth it!"

The cancer warrior at the center of this medical odyssey dances with her "dragon" of mortality through fervent journaling while telling a tale of great medical significance. As she wages war against cancer, her narrative wanders back and forth in time to excavate truths from her past, using her collection of personal journals as a tour guide.

While many breast cancer survivor stories have been published over the years, HER story is an original.

Original and inspired quotes are woven into the fabric of her character, "There is one thing in life that nothing can suppress... not cancer, not even death" (EMC) and, "The human spirit is stronger than anything that can happen to it" (CC Scott). Such epiphanies resonate throughout the book's beautifully wallpapered pages, like the first, second and third movements of a symphony. EMC's voice is both deeply haunting and hilariously captivating, witty and as wise as her Irish Grandmother, "Ginny," she so fondly characterizes. While exposing striking truths about herself, her family and "The Universe," the author's unique blend of profundity and sarcasm gives WIDE a lyrical voice.

And, in the end <spoiler alert>, EMC defeats the "Dragon" and extols, "Fairy tales are more than true. Not because they tell us Dragons exist, but because they tell us *Dragons can be beaten*."

While her story ends on a celebratory note, the reader can't help but wonder what lies ahead... Hints of deeply suppressed memories and family dysfunction are dropped like giant breadcrumbs throughout WIDE.

And the reader is left believing that cancer isn't the first dragon, nor the last, Elizabeth will face.

Will the author's aspirations of a trilogy materialize?

Our curiosity is more than piqued. It's burning.

Elizabeth Mary Catherine: 317 ... Dragon: 0

ISBN: 979-8-89175-001-2 (ebook)
ISBN: 979-8-89175-000-5 (sc)
ISBN: 979-8-89175-013-5 (hc)

THANK YOU for supporting a good cause.

Note to Readers:
The book's "Safety Video"

Confidentiality:

The author has the highest respect for her medical team and the brave women she met during her treatment. However, the names in the book have been altered to provide personal anonymity and respect for doctor / patient confidentiality, except where permission was requested and granted.

Discretion:

The information in this book is based on the author's personal experience, her recollection of events, and her interpretation of the medical research she did. This book was not intended and should not be used to provide medical guidance. Every patient's diagnosis is unique.

Commitment:

The author acknowledges that this book isn't necessarily an easy read. The journey wasn't easy for her, either. Parts are dark and tragic. Others twist and turn and are sometimes a tad complex. The author and her book aren't simple by any stretch. In the final analysis, she hopes the reader will find the book gratifying and worthwhile.

Dedications

For Virginia Mitchell Distel Schoenborn
A wise and refined lady who loved her grandchildren,
green beer on St. Patrick's Day and her books.

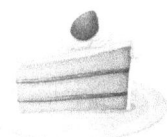

For Maria from Morocco
A brave and spiritual girl who deeply loved her husband and
son, museums on Tuesdays and bald karaoke.
Vous êtes mon ami êternel.

For Lillian Tartikoff
You are Living Proof
that the crusade against cancer can be won
and the definition of grace.
Thank you for making the world a more beautiful place.

For the Wise and Wonderful Dr. Melody Cobleigh
A remarkable lady who has dedicated her life to saving others.
You navigated me through uncertain seas.
This book is my humble expression of the gratitude I carry with me.

And last, but hardly least…

For Brian Patrick Grady.
The only man strong enough for me.
For your unwavering optimism and love,
and never ever, ever giving up on me.

Contents

Foreword

This book is based on a journal kept by the author during her odyssey with a rare and aggressive form of breast cancer in her 30's.

While this book is about cancer, it is hardly just about cancer because cancer hardly is. It is about the totality of a woman and the reflective journey she plunges into when confronted by her mortality through a choppy, sarcastic roller coaster of experiences and emotions.

And, as a "helix" wrapped around all of this, not to be eclipsed, is a story of *great medical significance*.

"L I V E   W I D E " is an expression of gratitude for those connected with the development of one of the 1st genetically targeted therapies for cancer: Herceptin. WIDE celebrates the long-term survivors who are a testament to the drug's benevolence over two decades later.

"L I V E   W I D E " is shared with the unwavering hope that we will someday find a CURE so that future generations will know cancer only as a constellation and a zodiac sign.

Prologue

Cancer has been a sinister enemy for centuries, a disease that is highly complex and difficult to treat.

Until the 1976 discovery of oncogenes – cancer-causing genes – the conventional approach had been to treat all cancers with a "one-size fits all" approach that was unpredictable in its effectiveness. The oncogene discovery marked a quantum leap forward in understanding the disease. By the early 1980s, scientists began to better understand the role some genes play in cancer growth. A flurry of research and financial speculation followed as biotechnology became an innovative means for technologically superior drugs with the glimmering promise of untold profits.

Leading the pack was a little-known California genetic engineering company that became the "overnight darling of Wall Street." Genentech's IPO in 1980 raised nearly $40 million and made stock market history. But Genentech was destined to make history in a far more meaningful way.

That same fall, at a Big Ten university in the Midwest, my mother was unloading me and my overstuffed Samsonite luggage in front of a college dormitory on the fringe of a sprawling campus. I stood in the shadow of the thirteen-story dormitory, comparing it to the three-story "tower" that was the tallest building in the "cosmopolitan" town of Gaylord, Michigan, where I had overstuffed the suitcases that morning.

What would a Wall Street biotech darling and a small-town girl who couldn't even win Miss Congeniality in a local beauty pageant have in common?

As my grandmother often told me, "Elizabeth, we all have a story to tell...."

"Life shrinks or expands in proportion to one's courage."

-Anais Nin

One: The Awful Possibility

(Frantically and partially scribbled on the back of a long Ann Taylor receipt ...)

Wednesday, August 26th, 1998, 10:04 am

I am negotiating with the Universe from the bathroom floor.

It is cold, hard on the knees and reeks of cheap vinegar. A stalagmite is sprouting in my stomach; my chest is crimson. Drops of sweat are tap dancing on my forehead. My right foot is throbbing from razor-sharp shards of glass lodged in my heel.

I'm on the verge of screaming out loud at the latrine.

I refrain, almost breaking into hysterical laughter instead and thinking, **"THIS"** is amusing. Amusing in a macabre, surreal, and cynical Stanley Kubrick-David Lynch-Woody Allen-ish sort of way.

Is **"THIS"** payback for all the fad diets I did as a teen, a tween and in my twenties? The freshman beer binges in college? Neglecting my spirituality? My ineffective time management skills? Placing too much importance on my career? Accepting asymmetry as balance? All the pain I inflicted in my failed marriage? Taking life too seriously and sweating the small stuff? For not flossing more regularly? Tossing the errant unmatched socks on my laundry room floor? Mixing paper and high-grade plastic in the recycling bin? Removing the "Do Not Remove" mattress tag? Not visiting my parents enough? Not being conventional enough? Not being grateful enough? And not knowing when to say enough is enough?

Make **"THIS"** be gone by tomorrow.

Please.

Thursday, August 27th, 1998, 9:11 am

Not so fast.

Sunday, August 30th, 1998, 12:07 pm

Today, I unpacked my shoe boxes of memorabilia in search of my old confidants: the worn, torn, and water-stained journals.

While I have been known to "journal" errantly on almost anything, from paper placemats, to the more cliché cocktail napkin, the back of receipts, shopping bags and etc., my collection of battered and water-stained journals serves as the single source of truth in my interesting and less than perfect life.

My first, with its frayed embroidered jacket and blue suede spine. "A Creative Recovery," the title page professes. An exercise in self-assessment when a creative awakening was my guileless life's greatest torment. Sort of a preface to the foreword to the prologue to an early mid-life crisis. I think the catalyst was Julia Cameron's reflective "The Artist's Way." In fact, I'm sure of it.

The second-born, dressed in a warped and tear-stained green cover with a cutaway revealing a Dragon Fly. "Creative Recovery: Continued," penned during another self-indulgent soul-searching period, the flames now fanned by Cameron's new book, "Vein of Gold."

"Journey of a Soul," my third. The ink is now so faint and blurred that my innermost thoughts live on as a slurred whisper at best. Labored over while living in the City of Angels, or as I dubbed it, "The Vortex." The journey of a lost soul on a quest for that elusive something. A search that collided with unthinkable consequences. The book's spine is permanently fractured and an image of a moon, smiling, mocks me from the cover.

Missing in action somewhere is Journal Three Point Five, sporting a glossy red veneer, like a Porsche roadster. Three Point Five made a half-hearted attempt to shed my Midwestern values and own my happiness when I moved temporarily to Los Angeles, but disappeared like California sand in a soft wind. That journal remains nameless and transient to this day, probably playing bongos on the beaches between Venice and Marina Del Ray.

And, "Full Circle," the youngest, with a forgiving soft cover. The inside of the optimistic canary jacket is graced by a Tom Robbins quote. The first entry chronicles my Midwestern homecoming. "Full Circle" was hell-bent on putting the pieces back together again. Yes, that was "Full Circle's" game plan.

My journals have always been my armor, keeping my most profound secrets and sanity intact.

This one could be my last.

As best as I can remember, the past three days occurred something like this....

Thursday, August 20th, 1998

I woke up late, like every other day over the past six months. This morning, how-ever, I woke up with a feeling. I felt heavier. Like I had gained five pounds in my right breast.

As I was blow-drying my hair, I dropped a brush and leaned down to pick it up, and my arm hit my right breast. To my surprise, it hurt. I yelled, "Ouch!" out loud at my cats, who were demurely observing the entire spectacle.

To my astonishment, through the steamed bathroom mirror, I saw my right breast was swollen and a little pink. When the f*ck did **"THIS"** happen? I placed my hand on my right breast. It felt hot. How odd. Maybe I have an infection of some sort? I've been in a rush in the morning lately, but how could I not have noticed this? It's like it blew up like a balloon overnight.

I lean closer, using a washcloth to smudge the steam off the mirror and get a better look, accidentally knocking a glass off the vanity. My pink toothbrush per-forms cartwheels in the air. The glass shatters over the tiled floor.

In the car, during rush hour, running late for work, on my cell phone, Dr. Tog, yes, he is the Ob-Gyn I see and, yes, uh-huh, yes, I did see him two months ago for an annual exam and a pre-natal consultation. That's correct. But can he see me again for, an, umm, some sort of...Swollen Breast Condition?

"Yes, he can squeeze you in tomorrow afternoon."

Friday, August 21st, 1998

As I was feverishly brushing my teeth, I began to wonder if I was behaving like a hypochondriac.

This "Swollen Breast Condition" is probably no big deal. Perhaps I should set up a consult with a female gynecologist instead, and this could all wait another week. Or three.

I notice remnants from the broken glass on the tile floor near the sink pedestal too late. A few shards pierce my right heel. I leave a trail of bloody footsteps down the hall.

I apologized to a few coworkers for not being able to attend the company outing. The office became desolate by noon, but I kept working diligently, almost deliberately missing my 1:45 appointment. I left the office late without my purse; a security guard had to be paged so I could retrieve it.

All collected, finally, I marched towards Northwestern Memorial Hospital. Like a good little soldier reporting in for duty. Ten minutes late.

"I saw you two months ago; what brings you in today?" posed the tan Dr. Tog. I sit up straight with my shoulder back and my chin high and eloquently describe my self-diagnosed "Swollen Breast Condition." Tan Dr. Tog pokes my swollen, hot, red breast a bit, furrows his brow and starts to look at me, sympathetically.

"Did you have *that* mammogram we discussed?"

"I'm not certain what you are referring to but I had one about seven months ago at Cedar Sinai Hospital in Los Angeles. Actually, Beverly Hills," I stated confidently, raising my intonation ever so slightly on Beverly Hills, throwing in a knowing nod.

Tan Dr. Tog doesn't look as reassured as he is supposed to, and I feel awkward having just come off more like a Valley Girl than a confident one. "I'd like you to have another mammogram, and I'm going to give you the name of two surgeons. I don't mean to frighten you, but I am concerned."

Concerned? How dare he...wait...what...Surgeons? I feel a violent rush of fear validating what previously irrational worries were. "Hang in there," Tan Dr. Tog says, squeezing my knee and exiting the room as quickly as he can without tripping.

What just happened?

I visualize the poster with "Hang in there!" in red bold comic sans typeface, a cliche fat tabby cat with bulging eyes hanging by its claws from a twig of a tree branch, as I stand abandoned in the cold exam room. Framed pictures of healthy mothers and cherubic babies are smiling down on me, from their secure stations on the office walls.

My trembling hands make it difficult to clasp my bra as I dress. As I study my reflection in the mirror, I reprimand myself and begin making an autumn mental to-do list. "Change out my summer wardrobe for fall this weekend." Brush my hair. "Go a warmer shade of brunette," I think. Apply lipstick.

Once at the reception desk, I politely and calmly request to make an appointment for a mammogram.

"Werner or Freedman?" The red-haired receptionist asks nonchalantly as if taking my lunch order. Her pastel blue eye shadow matches her eyelet cardigan.

"Um, whichever I can get into first, I suppose, is fine," I respond, matching her nonchalant tone.

"It's going to be a couple of months before you can get an appointment," Red-Hair Blue Eye Shadow sing-songs, averting her attention back to a Sudoku puzzle humming "Born Free" to the music wafting in the background. The receptionist power snub, as if I am trying to get a hair appointment at Christophe's in Beverly Hills with Christophe himself. However, I doubt Red-Hair Blue-Eye Shadow knows who that is. Deep breath.

Tan Dr. Tog walks by and heroically intervenes. "Immediately," he insists, and in an official whisper as loud and clear as if he was shouting through a megaphone, "This woman has SOMETHING."

Two other patients in the waiting room peer over outdated issues of "Parents" and "Family Circle," they pretend to be reading. I feel my left eye twitching. A few calls are made and they negotiate. They can fit me in next Wednesday at 9 am. Yes, that sounds lovely.

I put my sunglasses on and struggle to keep my lips from quivering. In the crowded elevator, I cower in the corner. For the first time in my life, I have an out-of-body experience. I am floating on the ceiling, watching myself navigate through the maze of the medical center. I look like a lost child or a rat in a lab experiment, small and confused. Suddenly, I am sucked back into my physical self again as I exhale with my entire might, violently shoving the exit door.

As if it was an escape hatch.

A flock of pigeons is startled by my sudden presence on the sidewalk and takes flight. I lift my hands to shield my face as if the sea of winged rodents might begin to viciously attack me. I can feel my face now covered in sweat. I visualize Albert Brooks in Broadcast News. I need to make it four blocks, four city blocks, to where I am supposed to meet Brian on an otherwise beautiful August afternoon in downtown Chicago, full of smiling, happy people.

BOOM.

A deafening sound fills the air as if an army of snipers is aiming at me from atop the John Hancock building. Another flock of pigeons flies in my direction; I lift my arms to shield my face again.

BOOM.

I step out onto the street, and an oncoming taxi comes to a screeching halt just inches away from me. I didn't even see it. I feel like a moving target.

BOOM.

Three Blue Angel fighter jets fly overhead in formation. Of course, the Air & Water Show this time every year. I am suddenly grateful for the distraction the Blue Angels provide so the smiling passers-by don't notice me trembling and weaving my way down the sidewalk on an otherwise beautiful August afternoon in downtown Chicago.

Somehow, I make my way to Greystone on Pearson Street, where Brian gets his hair cut. He has been coming to the same place for at least ten years. This thought is comforting to me for some reason.

I can hear Brian's voice, which carries so well, chatting up a storm with the stylist in the back corner. I see him seated in the chair with his wet curly hair and reddish complexion, smiling as he does so effortlessly. His blue eyes are full of life as he gestures grandly to the stylist, telling some humorous story in a cartoonish fashion that is a Brian Patrick signature. Such a happy-go-lucky guy.

Suddenly, I have this mental picture of myself dressed as the Grim Reaper hovering in the doorway. Electric currents start shooting through my body. I turn and rush to the ladies' room a few feet away. Lock the door, turn on the fan, run water in the sink, anything to muffle the wounded noises.

Freshly styled and smiling, Brian sees me waiting by the front window. I tried to force a smile; my swollen eyes hidden behind sunglasses. I must look like a mess. "The receptionist was very rude to me," I finally muster, half-hoping he will believe that was the problem.

"Everything will be all right,' he promises, as if that is a promise he can make.

At home, an appointment is made with a surgeon for next Wednesday, August 26th, following the mammogram appointment. I fill in the addresses and times in my Day-Timer very neatly and precisely. I announce out loud to myself and the cats with the utmost conviction:

"I've got **THIS** completely under control."

Monday, August 24th
The weekend didn't seem to have enough width to help me clear my head, so I took a personal day off, a rarity, to get my emotional house in order.

Catching up on the laundry was a requisite way to deal with the lights and darks, leaving no room for the gray. I first tended to a large load of white towels, warm out of the dryer and perfectly folded and stacked. I was carrying them down the hallway toward the linen closet when suddenly, the Blue House started spinning... out...of...control.

I felt a wave of nausea and remember weaving, grasping for a doorknob.

I awoke in a sea of white. I was grateful that the towels broke my fall, and, for a moment, I felt serene as I lay there in the white pile of terry cloth.

But tranquility vanished as quickly as it came and the Awful Possibility began searing through me like injections of fluorescent formaldehyde. I have never come in contact with formaldehyde. Why it would appear florescent or why form-aldehyde even popped into my mind? I have no idea.

Nonetheless, the Awful Possibility has a smell. An invasive odor. Sullied and sorrowful, as if life as I know it is decomposing. I curl myself tightly in a ball, feeling my hot breast burning against my chest; my heel is throbbing from the neglected shards of glass now deeply embedded in my foot. I buried my face in the towels and prayed the stinging sensation, the throbbing and the awful smell would disappear.

Through the screen window at the end of the long blue hall, I could hear shrill whistles officiating a high school football scrimmage and the smell of leaves being burned illegally. Charlie, the red-haired A.D.D. kid three doors down, is laughing and singing, ironically having a good day for a change.

I buried my face in the white towels to muffle the wounded cries I felt welling up from a deep place. From my fetal position on the freshly polished and lovingly restored oak floor, I studied what I imagined to be the long-tailed shadow of the Awful Possibility lurking in a doorway at the end of the blue hall.

Although I resisted it with every fiber of my being, I realize...

This is how it begins.

Tuesday, August 25th
I shower and avoid direct eye contact with the Swollen Breast. Maybe this insid-ious thing will go away if I don't acknowledge it.

I went to work like any other day. Except, today, I have an insanely intense intol-erance for the insignificant and unappreciated.

A Director of Corporate Communications from the client calls. At first, I thought he was calling to *thank* me for my recent effort on the not-for-profit campaign I helped launch. But, no. He was calling to draw attention to the fact that his last name was misspelled on the memo announcing it was being submitted for an industry award.

I feel sick to my stomach, like sour milk sort of sick.

I am further subjected to snide comments from co-workers and a frosty greeting from my boss because I didn't join the celebration of corporate bonding. I missed the Company Outing and took an unplanned personal day on a Monday, no less. How dare I have the audacity to address a potential health issue and go to a doctor's appointment instead? Shame on me. Where were my priorities? I feel my flush with disgust.

I have made meaningful contributions to the Wrigley business, a cornerstone account, in the short six months I have been here at BBDO, and I know it. Was I so naïve to think of my colleagues as friends who cared about me as a person?

Has Corporate America become this cold?

Brian calls to wish me a happy Tuesday. His brother has invited him to a White Sox game tonight. "I know you have your doctor's appointment tomorrow morning, but tonight shouldn't be any different from any other night, right?"

"I know you love the White Sox. I'll be OK."

I work until eight-thirty to pay my penance for missing THE company outing and for daring to take tomorrow as a personal day to have a mammogram without a response from my boss on the e-mail requesting it. Then I went home and fell asleep on the sofa after watching a fascinating PBS special on women with addictions. I woke up just as Brian is coming in the door.

White Sox win.

Wednesday, August 26th, 1998
I shower, avoiding direct eye contact with the Swollen Breast that is now slightly redder and oddly dimpled. I make the water ice cold, thinking that the sensation might reduce the inflammation and **THIS** might shrivel up and spiral down the drain.

No such luck.

When applying mascara, I deliberately avoid my bottom lashes.

I asked Brian if I could wear one of his shirts to the appointment. I choose his white tennis polo, which I match with an old pair of Bermuda shorts from college. Somehow this is comforting to me. I look like a throwback to my Alpha Chi Omega days at Michigan State.

"Go, Spartans!" I say to the birds-eye maple dresser and full-length mirror, mustering up all the cheerful spirit an alum can manage on her way to a diagnostic mammogram.

9:06 am
Brian gives me curb-side service at the radiology clinic on North Michigan Avenue, and the "thumbs up" sign, our private way of saying everything is A-OK.

I dutifully limp towards the old and grey building. Everything about the building is old and grey, including the security guard. As I fill out the insurance information, I notice a cobwebbed basket with brown wilted leaves, and a card proclaiming, "Congratulations on your new office space!"

And I remember an Erma Bombeck'ism..."Never go to a doctor whose plants have died."

I smile privately, trying my very best to be brave.

"Elizabeth Disco?" a mousy technician calls me into a cue. I don't bother correcting her: Distel, Disco, whatever. I visualize John Travolta, white jumpsuit and greased locks, looking all sultry and strapping, waving me towards the giant mammogram contraption as if he will be directing the photo shoot of my swollen breast. "You are ten minutes late," the technician announces loudly, for the record.

The Mousy Technician then proceeds to smash my red swollen breast like a pancake between the Plexiglas. "Smile and hold your breath," she instructs.

After several minutes that seem like an eternity, I'm told the pictures need to be retaken, and we may need to do an ultrasound. Then, after another tortuous few minutes of fumbling with the flimsy gown and pretending to read a two-year-old issue of Better Homes & Gardens, a different, less mousy and less friendly technician comes to summon me.

"The radiologist says more pictures won't be necessary. She wants to talk to you."

I suddenly feel like I might be getting the flu.

I excuse myself and make my way to the restroom. I lock the door, kneel on the cold, hard floor, and stare at the ceiling. The smell of vinegar is nasty. I rummage

28

through my purse and find a pen and an Anne Taylor receipt, on the back of which I start scribbling, capturing copious notes of how I am feeling. I have no idea why I am doing this.

From the cold hard floor of the god-forsaken grey lavatory, I begin to negotiate with the Universe. "I'll do WHATEVER you want!" I desperately bargain with the grey peeling ceiling, half expecting a response.

Silence.

"Please, please, PLEASE make "THIS" a false alarm!"

More silence.

Then, I began to hear what begins as a soft moan that grows into a slow, sad symphony of sorts, operatic, cynical, dark and tragic. A series of unfortunate notes. I pull myself up from the cold hard floor, shifting my weight to my left foot and leaning against the sweating sink. I study my reflection in the mirror.

The girl in the mirror stares back vacantly. I've never thought of myself as anything but average, really, average height, average weight. Well, maybe a few pounds above the "normal range" attributed to my thick German thighs. Average length brownish hair, corresponding brown eyes and average skin tone. Nothing out-of-the-ordinary can happen to Average Beth, I assure myself in the presence of the sweating sink and flickering fluorescent light.

I bid the god-forsaken lavatory adieu and obediently returned to the waiting room, doing my best to appear unruffled, calm, and cool while still futzing with the ill-conceived and ill-fitting gown. I wondered what lunatic designs these ridiculous gowns.

"Ms. Distel?"

The radiologist looks put out by my lengthy disappearance to the bathroom and is much less friendly than the Mousy Technician. Cynical, actually, like the lavatory symphony. The Cynical Radiologist opens the door to another gray room with two chairs facing each other. My films are displayed on a back-lit screen, and a box of tissues is strategically placed in the middle of the desk. The negative energy in the room is suffocating. Before a word is spoken...

I know.

The Cynical Radiologist moves her chair closer to mine and looks at me intently, with a lack of expression I hate her for. "This does *not* look good," she says, pushing the tissues my way and then gesturing with a sweeping motion over a smattering of white spots on my x-rays .

As if indicating the presence of a cold front or precipitation.

"Innumerable micro-calcifications (dramatic pause), as many as there are stars in the sky," she adds, in an unexpected and inappropriate poetic twist. I imagine her transforming from the five o'clock weather woman into a gargantuan slithering serpent with her forked tongue darting in and out and her tale rattling, waiting for the precise moment to…

"…99% of the time indicates…."

My body starts shaking uncontrollably, and I lift my hands in objection.

"No, that's not possible," I interrupt. "I just had a normal mammogram on January 16th at Cedar Sinai Hospital in Beverly Hills," with the same intonation I shrewdly use on Tan Dr. Tog.

I pause for dramatic effect.

"And a normal breast exam at Northwestern Medical Center by my gynecologist Dr. Randal Tog, *just two months ago.*"

The Cynical Radiologist doesn't seem impressed by my ducks all lined up in a neat row and almost seems to be taking pleasure in watching my ends start to fray with the promise that I might begin to unravel and plunge face-first into the box of tissues.

I pause and confidently inform the Cynical Radiologist, "So, *you* must be reading the films *wrong*. This is a classic case of a Swollen Breast Condition. That's all."

She shrugs, that's right, shrugs. "Is there someone I can call for you?"

"My ex-husband," I offer almost as a question, while the Cynical Radiologist tilts her head and looks at me with an arched eyebrow; as if that is the single most inappropriate response she has ever heard to this particular question.

"Oh, you see, we're living together and are discussing the possibility of getting remarried and starting a family," I feel compelled to justify our status for some reason, realizing how silly and perhaps borderline trailer park this all sounds. I remember Brian's number that I dial, on average, three times a day. I have to pull out my planner and look it up. She shrugs again, takes the number, and leaves me alone in the little gray room with my spotted x-rays and the tissues.

And then I see it mounted on the grey wall. My lifeline. I pick up and hit nine. Please, please, please. Dial tone. I start calling everyone I can think of. My mother. Answering machine. My boss's secretary. Voice mail. My boss. Voice mail. The department receptionist. Voice mail.

"Doesn't anyone answer their f@#%ing phones anymore?" I curse at the Kleenex.

I try the Director of Human Resources. Voice mail. Frantic to connect with anyone outside the callous gray building holding me hostage, I start leaving an incoherent message that includes clinic, radiology, more tests, and no reason to panic. Then I try my former mother-in-law, Nancy. She answers. She will meet us at Northwestern Memorial Hospital for the next appointment. The last call is to my father's accounting firm. "This is Elizabeth, his daughter."

I get put through.

Who knows what I said or what he managed to say? We were on the line for twenty minutes, and I couldn't repeat one phrase. All I remember is trying to keep the conversation going until Brian arrived. I'm sure there was some discussion of the weather and Notre Dame Football and how poorly Michigan State's team was expected to do this year.

11:15 pm
Brian arrives. We hug in a mannequin fashion. I smile in the same robotic manner and assure Brian, "I am fine. I had a normal mammogram seven months ago in *Beverly Hills.*"

We sign the release form for the film to take to the next doctor's appointment, and as I leave the grey clinic, the Cynical Radiologist hands me a tiny scrap of paper with "Y-Me" and a phone number scribbled on it. "They have support groups and resources. You are going to need support."

I accept this token of humanity from the Cynical Radiologist. But, I assertively state, for punctuation, in the direction of her lab coat as she walks away: "I understand that it may not be your style to sugar-coat your patient's results, but whatever the situation is here, I am going to be *empowered* by this." A bit startled by my words, I stop and look at Brian. I whisper so softly not even he could hear... "I have no idea where that just came from. I never talk like that. *Empowered* ...?"

But I'd like to believe the unexpected surge of courage was the Universe, responding in its own way to my passionate lavatory plea-bargaining.

We decide to stay downtown and walk-through Grant Park and have a leisurely lunch at an outdoor cafe, a luxury we'd never allow ourselves under normal circumstances. It's a beautiful day. On a scale of 1-10, we rate ourselves a 9.9. We are handling this so well.

3:17 pm, Lynn Sage Breast Center, Northwestern Memorial Hospital
Nancy is waiting there for us. She looks so pulled together. She even has a decorative angel pin on her blouse. I'm embarrassed by my disheveled appearance. The right hem is coming out of my Bermuda shorts.

Dr. Wilson Hearts III enters the waiting room we were escorted to.

He is toweringly tall and almost as tan as Dr. Tog. I size him up quickly and surmise Decidedly North Shore Dr. Wilson Hearts III, his petite blonde wife, president of her sorority at Vassar, and their 2.5 children must "holiday" in Bermuda where they all wear matching madras shorts.

Decidedly North Shore Dr. Wilson Hearts III asks all the same questions as tan Dr. Tog and Cynical Dr. Werber. I parrot the same answers and state emphatically that this must be a horrendous mistake because this is a classic "Swollen Breast Condition."

"This does look suspicious," he says as three needle biopsies are performed, two tissue biopsies and one, oddly, from my skin. I wondered why they needed that. I inform him that I have copies of my film from Cedar Sinai Hospital in Beverly Hills arriving overnight for his review.

"It'll just make you upset, " he cautions, implying something was indeed over-looked.

Results from the lab are promised Thursday afternoon. We're going to fast-track this. My assaulted breast, bruised, and stitched, is covered with gauze. It now looks three times larger than my left.

We go home and start making phone calls. Bad news spreads as fast as…

Mom. She immediately loses her composure. I can hear her shattering into a million pieces like a crystal vase all over the linoleum floor. Dad walks in the door before I can tell her that I am doing surprisingly well, given the circumstances.

Cathy. The middle and uber-competitive sister is the first to call. She humbly concedes that my pending diagnosis minimizes her struggles with the fertility drugs she has been taking. I assure her with all the conviction I can muster that I have this completely under control, whatever my pathology results. She makes a strange observation, "Beth, you sound more alive than you have in a long time," and offers to deliver the news to our dear Grandmother Virginia in person when she visits her later this week. The conversation is odd and rather matter of fact.

Jenny in San Diego. Her husband, Zach, takes the call because she is busy making dinner. "Jenny is upset." My niece and nephew, Kelsey and Colton, make happy little noises in the background. I ask Zach to reassure Jennifer not to worry. The conversation is strained and brief, as if it is an inconvenience.

Amy. My youngest sister is quiet. I stay strong, composed and upbeat. The oldest sister is supposed to look out for her younger sisters, not the other way around. But, she couldn't utter *one word* of comfort?

As the most awful day in my life comes to an unbearable end, the thin thread of hope I am desperately clutching to keeps ringing in my head...

This is just a classic case of Swollen Breast Condition.

This is the 1% of the time that the mammogram was wrong.

All those innumerable microcalcifications are benign.

Someone gets to be that 1%.

Why not me? Why not me? Why not me?

Thursday, August 27th, 1998
I feel like I'm traversing a deep ravine on a tightrope without a net, and the rope is beginning to fray.

A lab technician calls to reassure us that the test results will be given to Dr. Hearts III by two pm. They are not. Several follow-ups. Every time the phone rings, I jump. The medical business day ends without results.

The crisp fall night begins to creep over an otherwise lovely autumn day. From the porch on the perfectly tree-lined street, I negotiate with the Universe.

There is still a chance that I could be the 1% of the
time that the mammogram was wrong.

Someone gets to be that 1%.

Why not me? Why not me? Why not me?

I sat in respectful solitude, waiting for the Universe to respond…

Silence.

Friday, August 28th
The phone had an obscene and shrill sound when it rang.

I sat on the bed looking at the telephone with disdain, wondering if I don't answer it and if they couldn't find me, would this just all go away?

I slowly lifted the phone to my ear, half-believing the actual news might be anti-climactic.

The words instead have a stinging sensation that I had not anticipated.

"Malignant," "tumor," "large," "aggressive," and "invasive."

Decidedly North Shore Dr. Wilson Hearts III informs me of this in a gee-whiz sort of way, "We'll probably be looking at radical chemo right away. A lumpectomy doesn't seem to make much sense. There wouldn't be much left of the breast. We're looking at a full mastectomy here. And that's about all we know. Stay positive. We still have a lot to learn about you."

Fair enough, Doctor, so do I.

Off in the distance, the highway hisses in its omnipresent way, a siren wails, and from the high school marching band down the block, a singular snare drum rat-tat-tatting to the solemn chorus inside my head.

> *There is no longer a chance this is just a classic*
> *case of Swollen Breast Condition.*

> *This is not the 1% of the time that the mammogram was wrong.*

> *All those innumerable microcalcifications are not benign.*

> *It is official.*

I Have Breast Cancer.

I think this is the part where I am supposed to crumble to the floor, cast my eyes to the sky with outstretched arms and cry why, why, why or scream at the top of my lungs and hurl the phone at the wall or fall to my knees and begin to pray, if I knew how or to whom.

I feel wooden as I move unconsciously towards the bed with heavy limbs, my warm, swollen breast aching and my right foot throbbing from the glass shard still lodged in my heel. I begin to smell that awful suffocating formaldehyde smell again, which is even more invasive, sullied and sorrowful than before.

But now it is the smell of the Awful Truth.

And I randomly wonder...

Do I have to tell the cats? And *will they even care*?

Two: The Dragon

(Real-time again) Tuesday, September 1st, 1998
When I first learned about "the Cancer," just four days and a lifetime ago, I decided we needed a new Apple computer. We are now one of the first on our block with home internet access.

Today I embarked on a mission in this brand-new world of the vast web to search for personal survivor stories and the new advanced treatments I was convinced awaited me—just the antidote I needed. I plunged head first into the new frontier, anticipating the sea of comfort that would wash warmly over me.

It didn't.

It was like stumbling into the "Breast Cancer Wing" of the Library of Congress, if there were such a thing, but all the books were on the floor in no particular order. There was so much information in this alternate universe. I felt like Alice in Wonderland tumbling down the rabbit hole. I stumble through the complex list of search results, each report, abstract and article seemingly more distressing than the other.

The cold reality, I have found, is that treatment for breast cancer *has improved very little over the several decades.* Surgery, radiation, chemotherapy and hormone treatment in various permutations and combinations can result in remission but are not regarded as a cure. Sometimes, the patient will remain "in remission" for years, or indefinitely, if they are fortunate. Surgery does not contain cancer; it can spread from a microscopic tumor before it can even be detected. Chemotherapy and radiation are shotgun short-term "fixes" to the problem, bringing insult to injury and harming healthy tissue and cells in the process. And the last trick up the sleeve, hormone treatment, works selectively.

The most chilling statistic? *The mortality rate for breast cancer has not changed in the past fifty years.* Every year, an estimated 180,000 women in this country are diagnosed and 44,000 die from the disease.

Bottom line: Breast cancer is unpredictable. As are the available "treatments" for the disease. The cheerful pink ribbon I've seen pinned all over October might as well be an enormous pink question mark.

As I tip-toe through this webbed universe, I inadvertently land on a site that graphically depicts a "rare" type of breast cancer. Some of it sounds disturbingly similar to my symptoms and more horrific than I ever imagined breast cancer could be. I want to avoid the aberration I accidentally uncovered, but I feel compelled to read on.

Inflammatory Breast Cancer, or IBC, is a rare and very aggressive type of breast cancer that accounts for one to three percent of all breast cancer causes in the United States. It doesn't appear as a lump and is difficult to read on a mammogram. The clinical definition of IBC means that cancer has "invaded the dermal lymphatics," meaning it has already spread to the skin. This is why this type of breast cancer is called "inflammatory." The breast often looks swollen and red or "inflamed." In other words, "the Cancer" is already eating away at you from the outside in. Aggressive chemotherapy is the first line of treatment for patients with IBC and is called neo-adjuvant therapy because it is given immediately upon diagnosis. If they respond to the chemotherapy, patients undergo surgery and radiation. There are no accurate statistics on long-term survival for IBC. What is established is that recurrence rates for IBC are high. VERY high. For eighty percent of IBC patients, the cancer comes back within twelve to twenty-four months of initial treatments.

"The Dragon," I decided to call this most unfortunate flavor of breast cancer I randomly encountered, taking some degree of solace that at least I *don't have the most aggressive and rare kind.*

Here I come from a family of five educated, health-conscious women, and I had not so much of a clue that breast cancer could happen in your thirties. Or that not all breast cancer shows up as a lump. Or 85% of the cases have nothing to do with a family history. Or that treatments have not advanced and are unreliable at best. Or that "rare" forms could be so terrifying. Who knew?

Thursday, September 3rd, 1998
Who knew?

The Young Oncologist at Northwestern Memorial Hospital knew.

But she didn't offer it during our consultation. When I asked her pointedly if there was any possibility that some of my symptoms might remotely resemble the rare form I accidentally uncovered in my research, she said, in what seemed like a record skipping in slow motion, "Youuuuur ... caaaasssse ...woooould ... beeeee... caateeegooriiiiizzzzed ... aasss...."

As her mouth formed the words, my pulse stopped.

The words hung in the air like a noxious gas.

Then the weight of the following three words pulled every molecule in the room down to the ground with an astonishing earthshaking clatter.

"...Inflammatory Breast Cancer."

The Beast of all Breast Cancers... The Dragon.

Just when I thought I had hit rock bottom, I discover *there is a door in my floor.*

I laugh hysterically, thinking this is a macabre, surreal twist of fate. But, of course, why bother with a garden-variety type of breast cancer? The cinematic Lynch-Kubrick-Allen effect is brilliant.

After involuntarily sharing my unfortunate diagnosis and politely ignoring my inappropriate and curious laughter, the Young Oncologist innocently suggests I "consider" something the medical world refers to as a "stem cell transplant."

Hmmm.

A stem cell transplant doesn't sound so unnerving.

Well...in the online research "cramming" I have done in the past three days, in my novice opinion, they inject you with nearly lethal doses of chemotherapy, killing as many fast-dividing cells in your body as they can. Without actually killing YOU in the process. Well, killing you too quickly, I should say, because too fast is less profitable.

Having briefly scanned articles citing the Cancer industry as a $100 billion legal euthanizing business, I refrain from standing on the chair in the consultation room to give the Young Oncologist a piece of my mind. In that moment of realization, not only do I have "The Dragon" of Breast Cancer, but my life is now a revenue opportunity for a medical institution, I feel a tidal wave of wretchedness that hits me with such force that it nearly knocks me to the floor. With my head between my knees, while I began hyperventilating again, the Young Oncologist handed me a Stem Cell Transplant *brochure.*

As if I were planning a vacation.

I abruptly end the consultation. As I leave the Young Oncologist's office in a despondent fog, I imagine I hear a noise that oddly sounds like wheezing or a cough and see smoke oozing out from under the door of the Chemotherapy ward down the hall, as if it were a humidor. I think I can hear the Dragon snickering.

Friday, September 4th, 1998
Pardon the cliché and pedestrian question, but how can this be happening to me?

Diagnosed with advanced stage Breast Cancer at a young age when I had routine mammograms ten years before I needed to because they were offered for free on the company's medical plan. A routine mammogram just seven months ago and a regular breast exam by my OBGYN two months before being diagnosed with a ten-centimeter tumor. The most aggressive type of breast cancer for a health-conscious person with no family history, and the only risk factor is that I've not conceived any children.

A disease associated with a poor prognosis dumped in my lap just as I began to get my life back on track.

It is the definition of irony.

i·ro·ny1 ˈīrənē noun: **irony**

A state of affairs or an event that seems deliberately contrary to what one expects and is often amusing.

e.g., "The irony is that I thought I had immunity from breast cancer because I am too young, have no family history, and pro-actively had mammograms since I was thirty."

Synonyms: paradox, incongruity, incongruousness
Antonym: logic

Why does the Universe seem to have a beef with me? Who is steering the ship here, and are they asleep at the wheel? Evidently, "the Cancer" seems to be calling all the shots. And, for that matter, "the Cancer" will control every aspect of my existence for the foreseeable future. My thoughts will be dominated by "the Cancer" every minute and every second. Every conversation I will have will most certainly include "the Cancer." The first thing that greets me when I awake in the morning will be "the Cancer, and "the Cancer" will be my kiss good night before I attempt sleep and the thing that jolts me awake in the middle of the night.

There will be no rest or retreat from "the Cancer."

And I snort as I think that before "the Cancer," it was my career in advertising that ensured no rest. When my relationship with my family became distant, when once close friends had children, moved to the suburbs and faded away, when Brian and I separated the first time...and the second... and even when my marriage ultimately failed, Advertising made sure to it that I always had a full plate. And was never alone.

And, yet, here I sit very much alone, in the still of the morning at my trusty pine desk in a blue BBDO t-shirt and my pajama bottoms, staring at my Mac and the vast sea of medical information I have printed.

How does a woman with an Advertising background navigate complex medical decisions like neo-adjuvant chemotherapy, radiation, clinical trials, or a unilateral versus bilateral mastectomy?

No status meetings, brainstorming sessions, or call reports, just a plethora of information and critical life-altering decisions with no specific due dates.

And, as I listen to the omnipresent ticking of the 5th anniversary Tiffany clock, an idea slowly comes to me with a surge of unexpected giddiness or courage, I'm not sure which. I can roll up my sleeves and pretend this is a new business pitch. Borderline is brilliant! Now *that's* something I can work with!

OK, first things first, we need a code name! Because, of course, in the Advertising/marketing world, it is common practice to give "code names" to significant initiatives, new product launches, or confidential new business pitches.

Usually, the code names are "Project Batman" or something suitably silly. And I think of all the "Project Somethings" I have worked on in my busy Advertising career.

"Project: Kintaro," a new line of Asian-inspired quick meal solutions from Kraft General Foods. "Project: Verde," an environmentally responsible line of hair-care products from S.C Johnson that failed miserably because they were so far before their time. "Project Everest," code for a new Wrigley chewing gum with breath-freshening super powers. The list goes on.

All the project somethings I worked on with strategic finesse and fierce competitiveness, skills I will now apply to save my own life.

I make a new folder on my Mac: "**PROJECT: BETH.**"

I smile with satisfaction and proudly announce to the Tiffany clock, as one iconic advertising campaign claims...

"I am worth it!"

Tuesday, September 8th, 12:07 pm

PROJECT: BETH – Status Report:

Over the Labor Day weekend, I completed online research and developed an action plan which included multiple opinions from the best breast oncology centers in the country.

Still basking in the empowerment of being assigned to the most critical "Project Something" in my life, I was up at the crack of dawn, on the phone requesting appointments for second, third, fourth, and fifth opinions. Why stop at the second opinion when your life is at stake? There are "granted" based on the seriousness of one's condition. So, of course, I get right in.

The silver lining of having the Dragon is that the medical institutions treat you like a celebrity elite.

I visualize myself stepping out of a white stretch limo with Channel sunglasses, hair swept neatly back in a classic chignon, attired in something understated in pale pink from Vera Wang, sashaying down a carpeted walkway into the Mayo Clinic, waving graciously at the paparazzi, an adorable King Charles Cavalier poking out of an Ostrich Birkin bag, casually flung over my arm.

Anyway, I will spend an entire day getting "staged." They will take pictures of every organ and bone in my body to determine if cancer has already spread. The word is called "metastasized." The "M-word," as I refer to it, is just as terrifying as cancer itself.

3:17 pm

As much as I promised myself that I would stay emotionally distant and focus on my research and treatment like a "pitch," I know there will be moments of chilling lucidity. Moments? Whom am I kidding? But let's talk about lucidity, shall we? How can it be possible that little advancement has been made in the twenty-seven years between Nixon's declaration of the "War on Cancer" in 1971 and my diagnosis in 1998? "Poison, burning, and slashing" in this day and age of technology is still the best option and "standard of care?"

Chemotherapy, as I've learned, is highly toxic to the human body, with origins from a lethal substance used during the Cold War, known as "mustard gas."

That's right.

Autopsies conducted on soldiers killed by toxic chemical warfare in WWII revealed that the fast-dividing cells had been annihilated. Someone scratched their head and said, "Cancer is fast-dividing cells. Hey, let's use this *poison* on cancer patients and call it *therapy*. Brilliant!"

And so, it came to pass.

The thing about Chemotherapy that makes it so unappealing is that it is non-discriminatory. It kills any fast-dividing cell in the body, healthy and cancerous. Hence, the reason why patients lose their hair, become anemic, experience extreme nausea, loss of fertility and other "side effects."

And here is another fun fact...

Chemotherapy appears only to contribute a small percentage toward five-year survival on average. This was not posted on an accredited site. I'm also "hearing" this stat in the online support group I've joined, some of which include doctors and nurses with breast cancer. I'll take it with a grain of salt. But still.

I stare at the American Cancer Society website in dismay, disgust and utter confusion.

It stares back.

I defiantly hit the shutdown command on my Mac as if to turn off "the Cancer" itself.

I take a moment to survey my new "War Room." An overstuffed green sofa which takes up too much space because it was initially purchased for a spacious apartment in Marina Del Ray, flanked by a blue floral chair that doesn't quite belong. It too was acquired to fit a temporary apartment, during the first separation. A white-washed pine armoire that was a generous wedding from Brian's parents competes with the Asian coffee table that also looks like it is here accidentally.

Perhaps the Blue House's complete lack of feng shui is the reason I got "the Cancer."

My eyes settle on a framed black and white picture of my sisters and I, at a lake. I give myself permission to drift, just a little bit, to a time when "the Cancer" didn't command my every second.

"Emerald Lake," my Grandmother Virginia called it.

A floating dock in the green spring-fed lake became our summer headquarters growing up. Squeezing lemons over our heads to see how sun-bleached blonde we could get. Filling our bathing suits with sand as we did cannonballs into the lake to see who would lose her bottoms first. Diving to the bottom of the lake and pretending to be mermaids. Feeding our baloney sandwiches to the fish. Alpine yodeling contests across the lake that never ceased to entertain the Distel sisters for hours. Rowing the rowboat across the lake without permission. The sisters' chorus still rings through my head..."Let's get Beth to do it...*she'll do anything!*"

Indestructible, gutsy and carefree.

What happened to Carefree Beth?"

Did she die a slow death, or was it swift and sudden?

And as my mind drifts back to the cancer-filled present, I wonder *which is better, given the option?*

Wednesday, September 9th, 1998
Project Beth: Status Report:
Northwestern Memorial for "head to toe" scans this morning, to determine if the cancer may have already spread. This is often the case with an IBC diagnosis, I have learned from my online self-education.

They led me into a little room with an insensitive intern who asked me a series of questions including why they were doing such extensive staging. That's right, *he asked me.*

The attending doctor looked at the Insensitive Intern and enlightened him in a voice as loud as Tan Dr. Tog's megaphone, 'THIS PATIENT HAS INFLAMMATORY BREAST CANCER. THEY NEED TO KNOW IF IT HAS ALREADY SPREAD TO HER ORGANS AND BONES."

Honestly.

I am beginning to think there is ample business opportunity here: "Charm School" for physicians dealing with patients with sensitive diagnoses. I already have several in mind who would meet the eligibility requirements and would be happy to write a patient's letter of recommendation for the lot of them.

As I sat in the waiting room, however, my attention shifted to a headline on the front page of the Chicago Tribune: "FDA Approval Pending for Revolutionary Breast Cancer Drug Herceptin." At that exact moment, the top news story on NBC from the TV hanging in the reception area, "In a major scientific breakthrough in the treatment of advanced stage breast cancer today, a new drug called Herceptin is under review by the FDA, with approval anticipated for use outside of clinical trials before the end of September."

I have seen very little about it in my online research.

I took the long way home from Northwestern and drove through Lincoln Park. I thought about being bald, with one breast as the car weaved through the scenic park. Although I would not admit to myself that what I needed most was a gut-wrenching cry, the hot tears involuntarily streaming down my cheeks begged to differ.

I made myself a deal.

Once a day, I decided. I'll cry *once a day*.

Thursday, September 10th

PROJECT: BETH – Status Report:

Northwestern declined to commit to a due date for the scan results, which won't be delivered for another "several days." I get my dry cleaning back faster than that. The laissez-faire pace of some medical institutions floors me.

Confrontation with your mortality certainly shortens one's patience.

It also creates more urgency around things you were thinking of "getting around to." For instance, Brian and I were loosely planning to be remarried "sometime next year."

This past Saturday evening, September 5th, 1998, Elizabeth Mary Catherine married Brian Patrick. For the second time. In a private ceremony in the Grady's backyard.

The bride wore brown.

The family was in and out so quickly that it was a bit of a blur. And kind of a no-frills "drive through" Las Vegas-style wedding, only in Lincolnshire, Illinois, and no one was gambling or inebriated. And there was no Elvis impersonator.

I remembered our first wedding when we forgot to pick out our song, and "Close To You," by the Carpenters was assigned to us by the orchestra. Not exactly a song either of us would have chosen.

At the beginning of the ceremony, two acorns fell from a white oak tree. My father picked up the acorns and put them in his pocket. He believes in symbolism, he says, in his toast. He will save these acorns and put them in a box where he keeps unique things as a remembrance of tonight. (Long pause.) And he is hoping someone can tell him how to plant a white oak. *Brian is an oak.*

Those are the things he wanted to say.

Eloquent. But so odd.

Not one single word about his eldest daughter, the bride, who was just diagnosed with aggressive cancer.

Jenny, the sister who couldn't make the impromptu event because she had other pressing matters, sent Sunflowers.

In addition to the brown sun dress and sandals, I wore the requisite smile of a happy bride—reassuring every member of our "inner circle" that we were doing fine. We posed for family pictures, and aside from the mascara streaks on my cheeks, there was no evidence that "the Cancer" was in attendance.

On the drive home, I sweetly suggested to Brian that the *next time* we get married, we might want to give just a little forethought to "our song." Something by the Beatles might've been a good choice tonight.

Something like "Help."

The next morning before the sun was up, my family packed and headed back to Michigan, without fanfare.

My father dispensed his sage advice that I needed to stop procrastinating and just get started with chemotherapy. "The drugs are all the same," he asserted with his typical tone of authority.

Catherine, who had arrived in a pickup truck, loaded most of my LA furniture in the flatbed. It felt a little scavenger'ish in that moment. But none of that "stuff" was important and I was happy to let her have it.

As they all rolled out of town in a caravan, I realized how obligatory their visit felt.

Friday, September 11th, 1998

PROJECT: BETH - Status Report:
- 2nd consultation with Mayo Clinic today (via phone)
- 3rd opinion at the University of Chicago this afternoon
- 4th pending scan results, "qualifying" me for clinical trials.
- Called NMH; results not available, expected now Tuesday.
- My right breast continues to swell and is feeling warmer

- The skin on my breast is "puckering," looking like an orange
- New throbbing pain in my right armpit (or is it imaginary?)

2:18 pm
The University of Chicago doesn't know anything about the newly approved drug, Herceptin. Instead, they eagerly proposed a clinical study that is in the early stages of being tested. The study they recommended is a new protocol not being tested anywhere else in the country. It includes a combination of chemo and radiation together with a new drug administered at low continuous doses to increase the skin's sensitivity to radiation. They are in Phase I/ Phase II of the randomized study. You have an equal chance of getting the new drug or a placebo.

I felt my knees go a little weak when the Painfully Honest Oncologist ended the consultation abruptly, fending off my millions of questions about long-term side effects, with, "Our goal is to extend survival time."

While driving home, I heard another brief mention of "Herceptin" on NPR. Findings from a phase three clinical trial conducted by a genetic engineering company, Genentech, at some major medical centers were presented to the FDA…the result was promising…approval was anticipated within days.

How can Northwestern, a "world-class" Chicago medical institution, not know anything at all about what seems like a breakthrough in breast cancer treatment? REALLY?

I need to believe in a cure, as unrealistic as that may be for a patient with Inflammatory Breast Cancer. Every morning when I sit down at the desk, continuing my crusade to call every breast center in the country, I am feverishly determined to uncover that one tragically overlooked emerging protocol that will prove to be the most significant breakthrough since Nixon's War on Cancer, waged twenty-seven years ago. Maybe Herceptin is that silver bullet…?

Again, I ask, how does a woman with an Advertising background evaluate complex medical options like these? Having defined my adult life by a career in Advertising, I find myself so ill-equipped.

This is not like a new business pitch.

No, not at all.

Saturday, September 12th
Since I'm in a holding pattern until the medical business week resumes, I feel entitled to drift a bit. In any direction that leads me away from "cancer."

It is ironic.

The very thing that has defined my adult life, Advertising that is, began with a naive stab in the dark.

I was thinking back to the day I put the Advertising stake in the ground and I laughed out loud.

Some people may know from a young age that they are destined to be a brilliant lawyer, ground-breaking journalist, award-winning architect or a Nobel Prize-winning scientist. That kind of vision couldn't have been further from my reach as a small-town girl from Northern Michigan who wasn't sure what a "career" actually was. Far as I knew, people just had "jobs," which they didn't seem to like too much.

And my primary education certainly didn't give me a running start. Forgive me, but the Dominican Sisters who schooled me were more concerned about where the hemline fell on our plaid pleated skirts and how tardy I was for class.

"Free at last, free at last!"

I sang on the car ride from Gaylord to East Lansing on that autumn day when my mother dropped me off at Michigan State University. I felt that I had escaped from Alcatraz, leaving the Dominicans in my dust. I stood curbside in the shadow of the seemingly towering thirteen-story dormitory with everything I would need to survive campus life: a red plastic milk crate housing my Pat Benatar LPs, a couple of overstuffed Samsonite suitcases and my Clairol electric hot rollers.

But, oh, the slap of embarrassment I first felt when I discovered the other students arrived for their freshman year with something I didn't have.

Something called a "Preference."

I was soon to be schooled in the discomforting knowledge that the other students knew what specific kinds of classes they would need to take to get degrees that would qualify them for a particular career they had discussed and agreed upon explicitly with their involved and nurturing parents.

Like a simpleton, I stood in the assembly hall checking off the "No Preference" box on the fall term enrollment form, feeling alone and lost among a student population eight times greater than the town I grew up in. Surrounding counties and cows included.

That "No Preference" box would remain haphazardly checked for the *next two years*.

A wonderful period of self-discovery as a drifting undergraduate without a "preference" for anything except singing Frank Sinatra tunes at the top of my lungs in a dive bar called "Mac's" - a sanctuary for the in-the-know student body that embraced their preference-less-ness. The kind of joint where you bring a sharpie to leave your mark on the walls of the proud and preference-less. The type of joint where you check your inhibitions and morals with the bruiser of a bouncer at the door.

A semblance of a smile washes across my face as I recall the pinnacle of my guileless first year at the university.

Sigh...The Freshman Kiss. A naïve, devil-may-care adaption of the Hollywood or Paris kiss. Only mine was Gaelic, if the Irish can plausibly be categorized with those icons of romance. And in my book, they are.

Amidst all of the stumbling, sloppy preference-less patrons in that little musky matchbox of a bar, suddenly he appeared on a stool next to me... as if out of thin air. The Irish Wolfhound. Like a purebred who had lost his way and accidentally ended up in the dog pound with the unwanted strays. Disarmingly charming with an arresting smile and sky-blue eyes that spelled Trouble with a capital "T." Through the soft-focus lens of my Pabst Blue Ribbon goggles, the Irish Wolfhound looked pretty damn good to me.

And, as the luck of the Irish would have it, even better if you can believe it...the next morning.

As I was washing my face and brushing my hair, attempting not to wake the Irish Wolfhound, out of the corner of my eye, I saw that he was lying there quietly observing me and smiling as if I was a long-lost love he was surprised and quite pleased to see again. The Irish Wolfhound asked if I had pictures of myself as a little girl, which I thought was sweetly romantic. We took a long bubble bath, traded secrets from our past, and talked about everything and nothing in general while the world conveniently seemed to stand still.

He suggested sharing breakfast, choosing a quiet corner diner. We made small talk about silly things. It felt strangely familiar. I was wearing a striped t-shirt, my favorite jeans and a black leather jacket. Mascara from the night before smudged across my cheeks. He was wearing a wool pea coat and what seemed to be well-crafted Italian leather shoes.

But the lad could have been clad in a potato sack, for all I cared.

After violating the morning-after protocol into Sunday afternoon, the Wolfhound and I reluctantly said adieu. Like a gentleman, he asked me for my number and said he'd like to see me again. And as I watched the Irish Wolfhound disappear from my view, I replayed moments from our much too brief time together like an electric montage. Oddly, it seemed he could see through the barbed wire and steel security gates into the window of my soul. An unexpected connection so strong it might allow me to unlock that place...the place I had willed to be forever walled off ...so very, very, very long ago.

Freshman romances from Mac's Bar one-night stands were notoriously stamped with expiration dates shorter than library books. So I was surprised to find the handsome blue-eyed Irishman with the arresting smile was a longer flame than most. But the fire eventually flickered and faded for reasons that seemed out of my control. And others I will always regret.

The semesters blurred until that one-day defining day that shall live in infamy.

It was high time to declare my destiny.

I can still hear my thought process as I leafed through the Michigan State University curriculum at the firm urging of my academic counselor. I didn't get very far before I made a life-altering discovery while my inner narrative went something like this...

"Let's see, what would I be good at? OK, let's start with A's, *Accounting*. Definitely NO. My father, the CPA, seems pretty grumpy most of the time, especially around tax season. Okay, then... what about *Advertising*? Hmmmmmm, one can actual get a degree in Advertising? Advertising sounds interesting and creative. I'm pretty creative. All right then...Advertising it is!"

And so... Advertising it was.

Just like that.

And my young life's direction changed from "No Preference" to "Something Specific," like the well-mentored students from the big cities.

And as my thoughts drift back again to the Cancer-filled present, I almost laugh. I don't recall filling out the fall enrollment form for Breast Cancer. I'm pretty sure "The Dragon" would not have been my "preference" if I had.

Sigh.

What I wouldn't give to turn back the hands of time...to at least fifteen years ago...when I was indestructible, preference free and Cancer-less, listening to the Irish Wolfhound's charming brogue while soaking in a bubble bath the morning after making love that felt as right as rain and as if our stars had collided once upon a time in a land far, far away...when dragons terrorized damsels in distress.

And Cancer was but a constellation and a zodiac sign.

Monday, September 14th
I went to BBDO today. It's the first time I have been back to the office since the day of my terrible, horrible, awful and most unfortunate mammogram. I needed to discuss my request for short-term disability with my boss and the Director of Human Resources.

I still cannot erase from my mind the blank, emotionless look on my boss's face. "David, our CFO, kept working during his cancer treatments," he challenged me to reconsider.

For a moment of insanity, I pause and consider the challenge. Then, I returned to reality and that uneasy feeling of insult and disgust. "That was David's choice. Mine is to take the time I need to focus on my therapy and my complete recovery." And, then, for punctuation, "I have a new full-time job right now. It's called "Project: Beth."

I huffed and puffed right out of his office and down the block, and right into a Gold-Coast hair salon, where I proceeded to get, my long beautiful hair chopped off. Very short. For the first time since I was eleven.

This is liberating, I convince myself.

I continued my indignant huffing and puffing all the way back home with my liberated locks and a disability letter in hand only to be greeted by rooms littered with cards and flowers and a refrigerator crammed with "sorry you have cancer" casseroles. I collected the mail off the foyer floor to find a fresh batch of cards and letters of encouragement delivered this morning. I check my email to be greeted by another dozen cyber cards offering thoughts, positive energy and other appropriate words. I know the intentions are heartfelt, but yet...

I am alone in a dark tunnel without a flashlight or a map.

This is odd, I think to myself. Because this is a recurring dream, I have had since I was a young girl. Only my mother is standing next to me and I am begging her to show me how to escape. I am screaming, but she refuses to hear. She is looking the other way.

Why, in my life's greatest crisis, am I remembering this…?

Tuesday, September 15th, 8:12 am
PROJECT: BETH – Status Report:
Still no scan results from NMH.

I can barely stand the "weight" of the wait for the damn test results.

I'm about ready to pull my hair out myself.

I need a distraction, preferably one that isn't as high maintenance as this journal has become (no offense, dear Journal). To that end, I started carrying a little "Quote Book" book in my purse or pocket. Whenever I read something, hear someone say, or think of something profound, clever, or just plain "quote-worthy," I write it down. I have always had great respect for words. The more economically used, the better. Few things say more with less than a genuinely great quote.

One of the cards I received yesterday made my "Quote Book":

"Cancer is a word, not a sentence."

– Unknown

12:07 pm

This self-endowed liberation of a leave of absence is a double-edged sword.

All that space to think and contemplate.

Thirteen years of Advertising seemingly dissipate in a "poof" without a trace. Years of climbing the corporate ladder. Holidays and weekends working on new campaigns and eating cold pizza at midnight off paper plates within the confines of fashionable Michigan Avenue addresses.

Gone.

I gave up so much of my life to Advertising. What a foolish thing to have done! And what do I have to show for it now? A five-page resume. And one kick-ass coffee mug collection.

I enter the kitchen and open the cupboard to survey the coffee mug collection. There they sit, so proudly, little ceramic trophies.

A blue mug from Foote, Cone & Belding, where I started my career selling macaroni & cheese, tissues and other pantry staples, inscribed with "Advertising Agency of the Year, ADWEEK, March 1990."

A red mug from Tatham Euro RSCG, where I lost twenty pounds working for a psychotic director while pushing shampoo, aftershave and deodorant.

A green mug from Eire Partners, a scrappy start-up in a loft above an art gallery where we peddled anything we could.

A non-descript mug from an agency called Bozell that no longer exists where I slaved to sell Middle America fast food Mexican-style brought to you by a company in Irvine, California. Close enough to the border they ought to know better.

And the mug I deserve the most, the black and blue McCann Los Angeles mug. A keepsake for tirelessly toiling to consolidate brand assignments, as if millions of media billings might fill a void in my soul.

What wouldn't I give for all those years back now? I'd gladly trade in my Pat Benatar LPs, the Clairol electric hot rollers, my vintage Samsonite suitcases and even the kick-ass coffee mugs, for good measure.

Three: Ballistic Instincts

Wednesday, September 16th

PROJECT: BETH - Status Report:

Received my scan results from Northwestern. It took an entire week, but they are *all negative*.

No evidence of metastatic disease.

This is the first GOOD news since my most unfortunate diagnosis.

Since the neo-adjuvant types of chemotherapy they use are the "established pro-tocol," I've accepted it, as much as one possibly can, as a forgone conclusion. My first chemotherapy appointment is scheduled with Northwestern Memorial Hospital in 5 days, the soonest they can get me in:

> Monday, Sept 21st, 1998, 2:30pm
> Chemotherapy Treatment #1: Adriamycin Cytoxan
> Northwestern Memorial Hospital, 251 East Huron Street

All recorded very nicely, neatly, and matter-of-factly in my Day-Timer.

As if lunch with a friend.

However, despite this looming appointment, I am continuing to research medical alternatives and complementary therapies and trying to track down more about the new drug Herceptin that has received so much media attention. With due respect to the many highly credentialed doctors with whom I've consulted, based on the research I've seen, chemotherapy is a lifeline-extending treatment.

Not a cure.

I asked the Young Oncologist about Herceptin. She didn't know much except that it was just approved. Northwestern didn't participate in the clinical trials either.

I have been looking for information about Herceptin besides the little news coverage. I've started reading medical abstracts online, which is no easy task given my "vast" medical background. A doctor at the University of California in Los Angeles was heavily involved in the trials. Dr. Dennis Slamon has been pioneering this new research for years. It is something called a monoclonal antibody. They developed this antibody in mice and then humanized it to work in humans. In simple terms, the antibody recognizes a genetic defect in the cancerous cells and intercepts the "be fruitful and multiply" signals, so they don't. There are no harsh effects like chemotherapy, which kills all fast-dividing cells, cancerous and non-cancerous.

This makes sense.

Why hasn't genetically targeted therapy been discovered before?

On a side note, my sister Catherine told our Grandmother Virginia about my diagnosis yesterday over a ladies' lunch. According to the reports, she didn't miss a beat and said matter-of-factly, in between bites of her Reuben sandwich, "If anyone can get through that, my Elizabeth certainly can."

Also on a side note, a well-intending friend sent an e-card today with a positive message reminding me...." May your glass always be half-full!" To which I suppressed the urge to send a well-intending email reply, "When I pick up all the shards off the floor, I'll let you know."

Thursday, September 17th
Four days to "D-Day."

So many days, I would roll over, slam my hand on the snooze button, and wish I could sleep in and "play hooky" instead. Now I would give anything to be springing up at dawn, obediently following that cancer-free routine.

Instead, I'm sitting here at my pine desk, the autumn morning sunlight filtering through the blinds, reading more about the Herceptin trials and feeling perplexed by how little these fancy Chicago oncologists seem to know about it.

Could I be a candidate for the new drug?

I recall something on NBC about a doctor in the Midwest being connected with clinical trials. Nothing is coming up in my internet searches. I will start calling every medical institution in the U.S. until I find someone who can answer my question.

Wait, yes, UCLA Medical Center. I'll start there.

3:17 pm

Okay! I just discovered that a well-respected oncologist, Dr. Melody Cobleigh, participated in the Herceptin clinical trials through the Presbyterian/St. Luke's Medical Center here in Chicago. Herceptin works for patients with a genetic over-expression. You have to test positive for the over-expression to get the drug.

PROJECT: BETH - Status Report:
I have a phone screen Thursday with Dr. Cobleigh's nurse.

If it weren't for this new drug and the recent media attention, I would not have sought an opinion at Rush-Presbyterian-St. Luke's. It seems to live in the shadow of some of the other medical centers I've consulted with that seem to be more invested in brand marketing than cutting-edge research.

Friday, September 18th
Three days to "D-Day."

Carol from California called to wish me good luck "doing the hard drugs" in a couple of days and asked me when I said that I allowed myself to cry once a day, "When exactly do you cry? Is it in the morning when you first wake up? Or before you go to sleep at night? Or when you are sitting alone with the cats?"

I explained that my daily crying wasn't an expression of great sadness, actually, but one of being overwhelmed by life's magnificence at some moments. More powerfully than I have ever before. And, no, I don't cuddle with the cats. I don't really like cats much at all.

Saturday, September 19th
Two days to D-Day, just two days.

A well-intending friend recently gave me a copy of "Don't Sweat the Small Stuff." The book proclaims, "It's all mostly small stuff." The book also recommends you ask yourself this question: "Will it matter a year from now?"

In due respect, that's tricky to answer when you have a rare form of cancer.

Sunday, September 20th
The eve before D-Day.

I was up before dawn and went for a hard run. I sat here and stared at the key-boards, but the words will not come. I feel still, like the calm before the storm.

Tomorrow I will have toxic chemicals coursing through my veins that can cause fever, chills, blistering, infection, difficulty breathing, mouth sores with painful redness, swelling or ulcers, nausea and vomiting, diarrhea, irregular heartbeats, bleeding or bruising, hair loss, extreme fatigue, damage to muscles, nerves, memory, and cognitive function. In pre-menopausal women, infertility is likely to occur.

I recall a 5th-grade English class essay on courage. "It takes courage to admit you are afraid," I wrote. And I wonder now why a young girl in a small town that age wrote about courage anyway. Odd.

Little did I know.

My Swollen Breast is now dimpled like an orange, red and uncomfortable. And today, the nipple looks like an inverted belly button. I am watching cancer grow before my eyes and the defective cells might metastasize in this split second.

I'm terrified.

Monday, September 21st, 1998 5:11am
There is no snooze button to hit. I was up before dawn again and went for another hard run. I felt like I was running for my life. I skipped the shower because I can no longer bring myself to face the one-eyed monster. It is just too much to see a once beautiful part of my body morphing into something surreal and unrecognizable.

PROJECT: BETH - Status Report:
Northwestern confirmed the chemotherapy appointment

During our conversation, I mentioned that I was exploring a consultation with an oncologist with knowledge of Herceptin and could be switching doctors later, depending on the outcome. But I was informed that I could not see another oncologist for a consultation once I started chemotherapy treatments. "You can't switch horses during mid-stream," a nurse oncologist told me over the phone in a quirky, colloquial manner.

Despite the odd metaphor, I get it. I'm stuck until my treatment there is complete, or my condition worsens, and I again may "qualify" for a clinical trial.

How could I have missed this?

12:07 pm
PROJECT: BETH - URGENT Status Report:
I canceled my first chemotherapy appointment with Northwestern.

3:17 pm
Everyone is upset with me.

"You are delaying the inevitable," "Time is a luxury you do not have," and "All the treatments are exactly the same; you need to get started right away." And a few other pieces of advice dispensed indirectly by my family, when what I really need is a reassuring hug.

But, I get it. I have a hot, red volcano on my chest (formerly known as "my right breast"); the Cancer is visibly eating away at me from the outside in. I am a ticking time bomb.

What the hell *am I doing?*

I've spent the past weeks immersed in medical research and received opinions from the best breast oncology programs in North America that concurred that immediate aggressive chemotherapy is my best option. I don't even know if the new drug Herceptin would be viable for me or when or how it would be given. It has only been used on metastatic patients in clinical trials.

Am I stuck in a state of grief and denial? How does one explain that I am following "my gut" in a life-and-death situation? Or, is that precisely the moment when one's instincts must be trusted? My instincts are going ballistic and waving red flags.

And then I flashback to myself as a twenty-four-year-old girl on graduation day in a cheap blue dress with polka dots and perspiration stains, my Master's degree clutched firmly in my hand.

"THE ONLY PERSON WHO CAN SAVE YOU IS *YOU*."

– Unknown

Okay. We are going to do this my way and on my watch. And apparently whether I like it or not.

Tuesday, September 22nd
One day in the wake of the cancelled chemotherapy appointment, I was up before dawn again and went for the most challenging run in my life.

I sit at the pine desk in my sweat-drenched BBDO t-shirt, pulling out all stops to move up my appointment at Rush-Presbyterian-St. Luke's to see the doctor who participated in the Herceptin trials.

PROJECT: BETH - URGENT Status Report:
I moved the telephone consultation with Rush to tomorrow
An appointment is now scheduled with Dr. Cobleigh Thursday.

Soonest I could get, even playing the IBC card.

I've found more research reminding me that only some respond to the Herceptin drug. You have to have the specific genetic mutation, the "overexpression," I've read about to qualify for the very costly drug, which some insurance companies still consider experimental despite FDA approval.

Carol from California, who has a way of being wittiest in the midst of someone else's crisis, asked me this morning, "Beth? Who casually cancels a chemotherapy appointment? Will they charge you for it anyway, like at a spa or a salon? I know chemo isn't exactly like a hot stone massage, but aren't you delaying the inevitable?" This sage advice is being dispensed while Carol is, I imagine, sitting poolside in surfer shorts and a tube top, soaking up the California sun, contemplating a run on the beach or non-fat soy lattes. Or both, but in which order, later in the day.

On the other hand, I am captive in the House of Cancer debating the soundness of judgment I exercised in cancelling a chemotherapy appointment.

I'm sitting on the landing of the pine staircase, staring wistfully through the stained-glass window out onto the perfectly tree-lined street washed in scarlet, pumpkin and mustard. Indian summer is morphing into autumn, as the world is going on without me. The house is silent except for the tick, tick, tick of the 5th anniversary Tiffany clock and Charlie, the red-haired A.D.D. kid two doors down, having a not-so-good day.

Seriously.

With my three weeks of inflammatory breast cancer expertise, I bucked the established protocol for treatment recommended by three of the top-rated breast cancer treatment centers in the country and delayed my chemotherapy.

Just who do I think I am?

Today's Quote:

> *"It takes a touch of genius and much courage*
> *to move in the opposite direction."*
>
> – Albert Einstein (Genius)

I'm no Einstein, but I do have balls.

And instincts that I need to trust above everything else.

Wednesday, September 23rd
Everyone is still so distraught.

They aren't directly lacerating me for my reckless disregard for established medical protocol and seemingly irresponsible procrastination, but they are discussing it among themselves, the way my family always does. But no one is actually offering me comfort or help. Brian is immersing himself further and further in the busy world of Advertising, working longer and longer hours lately. I can't say that I blame him. Why be in a hurry to come home to the House of Cancer and the Defective Bride with the Molten Volcano Boob?

Hey…wait a minute…

That sounds like something I can charge admission for.

"Come one, come all! See the Bearded Lady, the Man with Elastic Skin and the Defective Bride with the Molten Volcano Boob!"

PROJECT: BETH – URGENT Status Report:
- I had the phone consult with Rush-St. Luke's
- I will meet with Dr. Melody Cobleigh tomorrow morning.
- We'll also meet the surgeon and radiologist to get a consensus
- And, at their recommendation, I will also see a psychologist.

My head is fine, I think. It's my swollen red boob that's the big problem here.

Today's quote by a woman who tells us it's OK for strong women to cry:

"Follow your instincts. That's where true wisdom manifests itself."

– Oprah Winfrey

Thursday, September 24th
Caught in traffic on the Kennedy for my consultation at Rush, running late, as I consistently do, I was terrified I might miss the most important meeting of my life. Why the hell couldn't I be on time just this once?

Suddenly, I morphed into a Chicago taxi driver, switching lanes and cutting other motorists off. I didn't mind the other drivers honking and flipping me off and thinking about getting a bumper sticker that says something like:

"I don't care what you think of my driving. I HAVE CANCER,"

or

"If you think my driving is bad, you should've seen my mammogram."

Brian is there waiting for me in reception. He came straight from the office and looked polished and handsome in his best slacks and a blue button-down as if dressed for Easter Mass. He hugs me and says, "This will be the right team for us, sweetie. I know it."

After checking in at the Department of Oncology, we feel "important" as we are ushered past a large conference room where all my x-rays and test results are displayed. A whole team of doctors is milling around and deliberating my case. Brian and I are led into a small waiting room, holding hands tightly.

Dr. Cobleigh leads the medical team in to greet us. With oversized glasses and wise eyes, she reminds me of an owl. An aura of calmness enshrouds her, like how dust surrounds "Pig Pen" from Charlie Brown.

I am in the presence of greatness and fight the urge to genuflect. "Wise and Wonderful," I think.

"I've seen all your pictures and lab results," Dr. Cobleigh says, immediately getting down to brass tacks, "Now I'd like to hear what you have to say."

Really? Four opinions from top-ranked medical institutions and countless more medical "dialogues" over the past month, yet not one doctor, nurse, or intern bothered with that particular question.

My response to that particular question? Let's say it will live in infamy as:

"MY MEDICAL MENTAL ENEMA"

Please keep in mind that "My Medical Mental Enema" was delivered in a manner as dignified as possible while dressed in a flimsy paper gown in front of at least five doctors and an omnipresent intern or two.

As I opened my mouth to speak, the totality of the past four weeks came spewing out with the velocity of a high-pressure fire hose in seemingly, to me, exquisite and elaborate detail…having researched nearly every protocol available in North

America for advanced-stage breast cancer, including most of those in Phase I and II clinical trials. I have a lot to get off my chest.

I pause for a second and consider taking a temperature check before proceeding. I decided the medical team might appreciate an update on the latest in the field of oncology. As I articulately regurgitated every fact and detail I had accumulated, I could feel the room dripping in the rich fount of medical knowledge I had cultivated. And I felt satisfied that I might have impressed these highly respected doctors with my self-conferred degree in Breast Oncology.

When I finally finished "My Medical Mental Enema," the room was respectfully and uncomfortably quiet. The Wise and Wonderful Dr. Cobleigh looked almost astonished.

"What is it you do for a living?" she asked curiously.

I thought I heard, "JUSTIFY YOUR LIFE, please."

I remember looking down at the floor, in that split second, realizing how insignificant my career and, for that matter, possibly my life to date, actually was.

"*Advertising*," I said apologetically, feeling professionally castrated, realizing in retrospect I really should have reviewed more of the preferences in the MSU curriculum book fifteen years ago. "Not saving lives like you are," my thought-bubble read.

"There are two types of patients," Melody responded, "There are "blunters," and then there are "gatherers." You are the latter." And (I think) she (almost) smiled in a refined, matter-of-fact way that made me feel that "My Medical Mental Enema" was, perhaps, acceptable under these unique circumstances. I hadn't wholly violated some sacred code of patient-physician protocol.

I imagine they had a clean-up crew scrub that room down with disinfectant later in the day, scraping away the residual remains of my Medical Mental Enema.

Friday, September 25th
After all, was said and done, I ended up at Rush-St. Luke's.

Attributable to the Wise and Wonderful Dr. Melody Cobleigh and her experience with Herceptin, a trusted friend's recommendation of the hospital and my instincts, weight averaged with other variables in the same workbook I saved a calculation of what "the odds" were in getting this diagnosis in the first place.

A random population of 10,000 times 12.5% of all women diagnosed with Breast Cancer in their lifetime, multiplied by 6% of women under 40, factored down by the 1-3% of all breast cancers identified as Inflammatory. That is about .00015, or 1.5 in ten thousand.

I wouldn't buy a two-dollar lottery ticket on those odds.

We will begin immediately on Monday, September 28th, at 830am with neo adju-vant chemotherapy, which means systemic therapy proceeding surgery. This is the reverse of how they treat the non-Dragon variety of breast cancer.

And, as soon as they test my biopsy for the genetic Her-2 over-expression that makes Herceptin work, we will know if I am a candidate for this drug. If I am, we will add it to the chemotherapy.

The protocol we may be following has not been used before.

"We will be sailing in uncharted waters," Dr. Cobleigh said in all her wonder and wisdom.

The waters may be rough, but I am tough, and I think I'd like to build a beautiful ship that will envy all the vessels on the high seas. And, as I know in my heart, I have made the best decision available; I can feel the yoke I've carried on my back like a beast for the past four weeks, leaving my body like steam off hot concrete.

And for the first time since the morning of my most unfortunate mammogram, I sense the faint glimmer of something I vaguely recognize as...Hope.

Coincidentally, all the major news outlets are heralding the news that offers Hope for so many women in desperate need of it.

Like me.

The FDA approved Herceptin today.

Biotechnology Breakthrough in Breast Cancer Wins FDA Approval

New Therapy for a Quarter of Women with Metastatic Breast Cancer; Testing for Protein Over-Expression Critical

SOUTH SAN FRANCISCO, Calif., - September 25, 1998 – Genentech, Inc. (NYSE: GNE) announced today that it received approval from the U.S. Food & Drug Administration (FDA) for Herceptin® (Trastuzumab), a unique new approach for treating one type of metastatic breast

cancer and the first monoclonal antibody for use in this disease. In October, the new biologic drug will be available through the oncology medical community."

Maybe, the proverbial glass has a few drops of something left in it.

As opposed to being shattered all over the floor.

Four: Chemopolous

Monday, September 28th, 12:07pm
Dearest Journal, today was more than a tad surreal, so the best way to tell it is like a mashed-up film-noir-meets-today's-Hollywood-story-tale, of sorts, and quickly. While I still feel well.

I, the Defective Bride, arrived predictably ten minutes late and stood steadfast at the gates of Rush-St-Presbyterian's Medical Center, with my molten volcano breast staring bravely into the city of Chemopolous.

Ding-dong and hip, hip hurray, long live C-Day.

The room was respectfully quiet except for muffled coughs and sneezes here and there; I could hear a syringe drop in the next room. The metropolis was over-crowded with reclining thrones, decorative boxes of Kleenex and plastic perennials adorning the side tables.

The head nurse holding court at the gate raised her head from the "reservation list" she was micro-managing as if strategically deciding where to seat Sylvester Stallone at Matsuhisa in Aspen during the Sundance Film Festival. If the festival were held in Aspen, that is.

The Queen of Chemopolous, I dubbed her.

Except for her tortoise framed glacier blue eyes, The Queen of Chemopolous was as monochromatic and shrouded in a soft 30- watt luminescence. And as I silently prepared for chemical warfare, I nobly lifted my gaze to meet that of The Queen's while half curtsying. She subtly tilted her head and looked at me with her tortoise framed glacier blues, kindly and quizzically, as if I've wandered into the wrong room.

I liked her instantly.

The Queen of Chemopolous struck me as a mélange of Florene Nightingale, Gilda the Good Witch and Marlene Dietrich, sans cigarette. Her presence added a touch of retro glam to the respectfully quiet metropolis. Porcelain complexion and sinewy stature, I imagined her doing the breaststroke among the reclining thrones, her snow-white locks tucked up in an ivory bathing cap, emanating all the style and grace of Ester Williams. She could pull off a pair of stilettos with that uniform, I thought, distracting myself from the bitter business close at hand.

"Your name?" she almost cooed as her glacier blues continued to inspect the crowded "guest list" smudged with eraser marks and detailed with footnotes. Such a popular place.

"Beth Distel. It could also be under Elizabeth." I offered helpfully. It felt appropriate to use my complete given name when addressing The Queen.

She looked at me vacantly with her glacier blues as if I was not on the "A-List," at all. "I mean Grady. Try Grady...perhaps, Distel-Grady or maybe it is under Grady-Distel, for that matter...." I blurted out nervously.

She tilted her royal head and studied me as if I was speaking in gibberish. I feel like a court jester failing to amuse the Queen.

"There's a story here, but the short of it is that I'm here for my first Chemotherapy," I explained.

"We will find you a nice private spot next to the window." As if she was waving a wand, the Queen of Chemopolous gestured towards a pale blue vinyl recliner in a sunny corner with a side table sporting a vase of plastic peonies and the requisite decorative box of Kleenex. She raised a perfectly arched eyebrow, awaiting my approval.

"That's nice." I tried to smile, to let her know how much her regal touch of kindness meant.

"Kelley, can you escort Elizabeth to station three?" The Queen of Chemopolous discharges one of the new interns. The Fresh Intern looks up at me with eyes as big as saucers. She must be all of twenty-two.

I am suddenly aware of eyes following me as we navigate back to the sunny corner of the metropolis. "The Eyes" pretended to be obsessed with their knitting, crocheting, and Reader's Digests. I felt like an intruder in Chemopolous, which I'd prefer not traverse thank you very much. I noted that I was the only young patient in the room. My presence makes "The Eyes" uncomfortable, I think. They seemed to be studying me, seemingly wondering what I may have done to bring this upon myself. I can almost hear their thought bubbles ...*I'll bet she did recreational drugs. Perhaps cocaine. Perhaps she smoked cigarettes. A pack a day.*

I averted my attention from "The Eyes" and the imaginary tapestry of judgment to a table with pamphlets and brochures displayed matter-of-factly. "Take-One!" the sign cheerfully suggests. These "take-ones" enumerate the common side-effects of Chemotherapy I've read about. Seeing them in a "brochure" is surreal.

Persistent nausea and vomiting, diarrhea, fast or irregular heartbeats.
Unusual bleeding or bruising, hair loss, blood in your stools, or urine.
Extreme fatigue, unable to carry on self-care activities.
Closing up of the throat, swelling of facial features, hives.
Mouth sores with painful redness, swelling, or ulcers.
Fever, chills, infection, shortness of breath, wheezing, difficulty breathing.
Damage to the muscles and nerves, affecting memory and cognitive function.
In pre-menopausal women, infertility is likely to occur.

I place my randomly selected "brochure" back in its slot. I don't "take one."

I take a seat in the chair and I feel my heartbeat quicken.

I wonder if this is how a convict might think as he, or she, prepares to face lethal injections. The Fresh Intern puts a tight rubber band around my left arm, and I clench my fist. I close my eyes, and a sharp pain surges through my hand as the catheter is put into place.

"First, I'll give you a shot of Benadryl that will make you sleepy and relaxed, then I will give you the Adriamycin, which is the red bag, and then you will get a bag of saline to flush the drugs through your system. This will take about two hours. Can I get you something to read? Would you like some lemon drops? Some of our patients like them because they help you from getting a dry mouth." The Fresh Intern looks up at me, hopefully with her big saucer eyes, as if the suggestion of lemon drops might be enticing.

As the first wave of drugs began coursing through my veins, I looked out the window at the most distant point I could find on the skyline. I imagined tall waves on the horizon and something resembling a pirate ship mast. I could almost hear the distant ringing of her cannons firing at shore batteries as she surges boldly forward and the echoes secede into slow, haunting music, like a wind-up snowglobe. I blinked back the welling tears and promised myself there will be no watershed as the skyline became more obscured and my thoughts more slurred.

I drift off into a drug induced sleep, imagining white loons taking flight over vast fields of black daisies.

Tuesday, September 29th
Good morning, Vietnam. Please pass quickly.

Wednesday, September 30th
I hadn't felt that wonderful since the morning after I drank tequila shots for the first time as a freshman at MSU on an empty stomach and then spent the night in the back of my roommate's orange Ford Pinto. My "friends" proceeded to cart me around until 4 am on their not-to-be-interrupted bar-hopping mission.

The morning after Chemopolous was spent in the fetal position on the couch, where I listened to classical music and contemplated boiling water. I promised myself I would not let the chemotherapy hangover keep me down. I tried to stand. But the best I could do was to put one foot on the floor. The cold wood floor against my food was oddly comforting. I lay there in that position for hours, wistfully daydreaming of being able to put both feet on the floor and walking to the kitchen to make a cup of green tea.

But now that a few days have passed, I'm regaining my strength.

The more I read about chemotherapy online, the more I hope I test positive for HER2. As positive as possible. Which is counter-intuitive since the most aggressive breast cancer is the HER2-positive type. I have learned that the human epidermal growth factor receptor 2 (HER2) helps breast cancer cells grow. Herceptin works by targeting HER2 proteins to stop cancer cell growth. The benevolent drug is associated with cases of complete remission in women who were stage four for a very long time.

This HER2 business is fascinating to me.

Someone should write a book about the development and trials of Herceptin.

Far be it from me, with my self-conferred oncology degree, to be posing hypothetical questions, but it seems like they are only beginning to understand the role of HER2 in breast cancer. For example, would patients live longer by treating them with Herceptin and chemotherapy earlier – before their cancer becomes metastatic and spreads to other parts of the body?

Patients like me.

What are the odds that I could be diagnosed with IBC and be HER2 positive but receive this most unfortunate diagnosis just as the FDA approves a breakthrough treatment that works on that specific genetic mutation AND somehow find my way to one of the best oncologists in the country with unparalleled experience with the new drug?

Decidedly less than one in a million.

We will know in about a week if my biopsy tested HER2 positive. There is a twenty percent chance that I might have the "over-expression." Those sound like BIG numbers to me.

All things considered.

Thursday, October 1st

Cancer by numbers, Dear Journal, turns out, not so much fun. I'm putting the spreadsheets and statistics out of my head because, whatever my results are, they will be one hundred percent representative of me.

I have a full three weeks before I'm back for round two of my hardcore drugs, and I've decided to indulge myself and do whatever I want to do with my newfound freedom. And so, I've decided to journal today and let the words transport me far, far away.

Someplace where Cancer would never think to look for me.

Back in the days when "the odds" were something I only thought about when buying a lottery ticket, which I never did because I actually once believed in "the odds." Simpler days, like when one's compass is set, one has a "Preference," and one can run like the wind. Days made of Big Ten football rivalries, TGIF happy hours and term parties. Most of which I declined and studied through, playing catch up with all the other well-mentored big-city students.

How excited and proud I was when I received the letter from the Dean informing me that I had been awarded a scholarship in the Master's program in Advertising.

The near-poverty-level lifestyle I could afford on a Teacher's Assistant stipend and late-shift waitressing tips led me to a studio apartment on the fringe of the campus, which I shared with my roommate, the nymphomaniac. I would spend the next two years entering our humble pied-a-terre with great trepidation, wondering which "Mystery Date" I might meet. But my near poverty-level lifestyle with the sex-crazed roommate seemed inconsequential the day I was to receive my Master's degree.

I remember every detail of that day, like a scene from an old classic movie that you know line by line, frame by frame. I remember…stripping out of my waitress uniform in the break room at Winn Schuler's, a family restaurant where I worked weekends and evenings for modest tips…pulling my wrinkled little blue polka dot dress out of my backpack…pedaling to the assembly hall like a bat out of hell… donning my cap and gown…taking a seat next to my classmates…suddenly conscious of the perspiration stains on my cheap blue dress…the smell of the deep fat fryer and Winn Schuler's world-renowned "Bar-Scheese" on my hair…

And two empty seats behind me.

I can still taste the wave of disappointment that washed over me when the university president asked us to give a standing ovation to the people who made this possible: our parents.

Mine had always been clear with me that higher education was a luxury, and not one they intended to help me with. Nonetheless, I felt abandoned at that moment. But the dampness of disappointment was quickly lifted and replaced by an intense rush of pride as I walked across that stage. I clutched that diploma like a sprinter as if I were handed an Olympic baton. It might have been my imagination, but the applause when my name was read seemed especially thunderous. Like the Universe was giving me a private salute.

I bicycled back to the restaurant after the commencement ceremonies. I masked the embarrassment I felt as I served dinner to the other graduates celebrating with their smiling families later that day.

That blend of accomplishment and humility I will never forget was an epiphany that has defined me since.

I could count on Beth.

Little did I know then how valuable that self-reliance would eventually become.

"Don't compromise yourself. You're all you've got."

– Janis Joplin

Friday, October 2nd

Speaking of commencements, now that the initial medical decisions have been made and treatment has commenced, there isn't much to do but drink green tea, meditate, eat a macrobiotic diet, pop anti-nausea pills, process insurance forms, abstain from doing more research on IBC survival rates, focus instead on learning more about Herceptin, take long walks to keep up my strength, look forward to my hair falling out, wait for my HER2 test results and write.

And contemplate the meaning of life.

And so, today, I'll choose to write…about a simpler life…in which attending my college graduation ceremony alone seems like my life's greatest travesty, the smell of Winn Schuler's world-renowned "Bar-Scheese" still heavy on my hair.

If you look up the definition of "awkward" in Webster's, I'm pretty sure you'd find to this day:

awkward, adjective: awkward

1. Not smooth or graceful; ungainly, e.g., "Young naïve Beth was so awkward in interviews with the crème de la crème advertising agencies from Detroit, Chicago and New York you would cringe with embarrassment for her."

Synonyms: clumsy, ungainly, uncoordinated, graceless, inelegant, gauche, gawky, wooden, stiff

How badly I bumbled through interviews with Dancer-Fitzgerald and W.B. Doner and completely humiliated myself with Leo Burnett's pickiest shiny-shoed recruiter. I was late to the interview and said all the wrong things, like the reason I chose advertising as a major is because I didn't think I'd be good at accounting.

How deflated I felt when I realized my academic accomplishments may have been for naught as I was quickly passed by for the more poised candidates despite my excellent grades. I contemplated going straight on to get my Ph.D., a program to which I was accepted and awarded a fellowship but to which I was advised to decline as I would be over-educated and inexperienced and would find it next to impossible to secure employment with a Ph.D. at such a young age.

That advice was the only academic/career guidance my father, the accountant, ever doled out to me.

Stepped over but hardly squashed, I felt adrenaline packing my few worldly possessions and hitching a ride to Chicago, hoping to secure some form of employment.

Advertising or otherwise.

Just me, my diploma, Clairol electric hot rollers, Pat Benatar now crammed into the plastic red milk crate with The Who, Jimmy Hendrix and Frank Sinatra, my trusty overstuffed Samsonites and my new friend, the Wooden Stool.

The Wooden Stool was a by-product of the K-Mart shopping spree my mother generously treated me to when I moved into the studio apartment with my room-mate, the sex addict.

"You can choose anything you'd like for your new apartment," my mother offered in a pathetic attempt to help me feather my grad school pied-a-terre. Amidst the high-end K-Mart home accessories, the Wooden Stool looked alone and plain, just like I felt at the time.

A decade later, the Wooden Stool has moved with me at least seven times.

At one time, buying a piece of furniture at K-Mart was a significant life decision. Now I get to choose which recliner I'd prefer to sit in to have toxic chemicals coursing through my veins while conjuring visions of pirate ships and endless fields of Black Daisies.

I wonder *why* these images keep running through my head.

Five: A Parachute That Might Work

Saturday, October 3rd

Dear Journal, I've decided that the absolute cruelest thing the Universe could give to an introspective person is " The Cancer."

I gave up on religion at thirteen. I remember this precisely because I had just lost my virginity, which opened the door to questioning everything. I was a bona fide woman and could no longer run around blindly accepting things at face value.

Here I sit, twenty-three years later, in need of some faith.

There has to be something more than this.

I turn it over and over, and I have a new revelation which goes pretty much like this:

The meaning of life is too profound to be known and understood.
Man accepts the reality with which he is presented.
This is why common religion has put a human face on "God."
The more meaningful existence defies comprehension.
This is where faith comes in.
Our soul/ inner energy must go through a series of lessons
to prepare it for a higher level of existence.
Although human life is a temporary passageway, it is a great gift.
Happiness and love are meant to be enjoyed and shared.
Life provides our souls with the means to help other others.
That is an essential part of the lesson.
We are all connected.
Energy never dies.
And love is far too powerful to be transient.

Life must be more than a random result of fission.

Because, if this is all there is, facing my mortality is an entirely different proposition.

Isn't it?

Sunday, October 4th

I solved the mystery of life yesterday.

In fewer words than it took me to describe my college graduation day.

Breast cancer really is empowering.

Monday, October 5th

PROJECT: BETH - Status Report:
- Pathology confirms I exhibit HER2 solid over-expression.
- Qualified to receive bi-weekly Herceptin infusions.
- Strongly "ER positive."
- 1st Herceptin infusion is Wednesday, October 14th.

I can't help but be struck by the fact that then years ago, the HER2 over-expression was dire news. Today, a mere ten days after the FDA approval of Herceptin, there is a possibility I could have a dramatic response to this antibody.

So, I suppose this is the best bad news I could expect.

I make a note in my trusty quote book:

"The bad news is…you are falling through the air.

The good news is…you have a parachute…that _might_ work."

– Some Seriously Cynical Optimist.

(Pause)

Brian just called from work to find out the HER2 test results. I told him that Cobleigh said my HER2 over-expression was the strongest she had seen. And I told him I thought this was the best bad news we could have possibly hoped for. This was met by silence on the other end of the line. I could feel his fear over the phone. "That's great, sweetie…" he said in a fabricated upbeat tone, and then he had to rush off to a meeting.

I wish I had a meeting I had to rush off to. Instead, I'm stuck playing the role of the Defective Bride in the House of Cancer with my debonair co-star, the Dragon.

When we hung up, I sat on the kitchen floor and cried until I had nothing left inside.

Tuesday, October 6th

I've decided to be genuinely, positively, and unflinchingly optimistic about my HER2 over-expression.

It's my best and only option.

And while there is still so much we don't know about the drug and how it interacts with traditional chemotherapy, how well it benefits a patient with IBC or what to expect in the neo-adjuvant setting, it has shown remarkable results for many women in the clinical trials. I need to believe with that the parachute will unfurl with breathtaking splendor.

While I bide my time waiting for my new parachute, I think I have earned the right to meander back in time again. Yes, I think I'd gladly trade in both breasts to return to those uncomplicated days of being young and invincible.

It was gratifying to finally be employed by a prominent Chicago advertising agency without "inside connections" and an expensive suit. How proud I was when I received my first promotion at Foote, Cone & Belding. On top of that, I was thrilled to be living in what I consider the best city in the world. Inhaling all that it had to offer.

Especially the social opportunities.

"The Lust Barge," the invitation read.

It was the party of the summer and everyone who was anyone in the Chicago advertising world set sail aboard the Lust Barge that night. I climbed aboard in white cotton sailor pants and a nautical-striped sweater with a fistful of business cards just waiting to be put into the right hands.

As the pink sun began to sink behind Chicago's skyline and the plastic cups of cheap chardonnay flowed freely, the ostensible networking became unapologetically social.

Inevitably, I found myself enchanted by an Irishman.

"Fat Freddie," they called him.

Fat Freddie was belting out rude lyrics to otherwise romantic ballads. I was the only girl on the Lust Barge who wasn't offended and was enjoying his inappropriate serenade. And then, I noticed another Irishman, a little less imposing than Fat Freddie. His blue eyes locked with my brown eyes, and he smiled enthusiastically as he extended his hand and said, "Well, if you think he's funny, maybe I have a chance at making you laugh, too!"

And make me laugh, Brian Grady did.

Brian worked in advertising like me. He was from a respectable Midwestern Catholic family, like me. He liked to jog, like me. He was artistic and creative, like me. Brian was, in fact, a lot like me. He showed me the city I was so new to and courted me as if his life depended upon it.

Those were happy days.

How was it that everything got so horribly off track?

Wednesday, October 7th
It is just one long month and ten days, to be exact, because I always am, from the night I felt the world shifting underneath my feet.

I don't know what made me start recording my feelings and the events, beginning with the first entry on the back of the Ann Taylor receipt in the bathroom of the radiology clinic on the day of what will forever be known as my most unfortunate mammogram. Despite my fear of what else I might predict, I believe in the medicinal powers of journaling.

So, I keep writing.

And I keep questioning.

In the grand scheme of things, *why are we here?*

To chase dreams, to live dreams, to realize our potential? To be happy and flourish? To become the person you are destined to be if destiny is a thing? To achieve physical perfection? To expand our horizons? To live in each moment, free from the last? To survive as long as possible in pursuit of immortality through scientific means? In other words, to live forever or die trying? To eat, drink, and be merry? To give more than you take? To be fruitful and multiply? To know as much as possible about as many things as possible? To lead, follow or get out of the way? To leave an imprint that wouldn't have been there should you not have lived at all? To turn the other cheek? To buy the world a home and furnish it with love? To grow apple trees and raise snow-white turtle doves? To face our fears? To rule the world? To do the right thing? To shine our life like a light? To slip out the back, Jack? To be understood and to understand? To smile on your brother and help one another right now?

What if Life has no meaning?

What if Life or human existence did occur out of a random chance in nature, and anything that exists by chance has no intended purpose? What if there is no point in Life, and that is precisely what makes it so unique? In that case, the Meaning of Life is to forget about the search for the Meaning of Life.

And just live it.

For as long or as short as we get.

Thursday, October 8th
I've just discovered that someone DID write a book about Herceptin,

"HER-2: The Making of Herceptin, a Revolutionary Treatment for Breast Cancer." It was published in August, the day before my awful mammogram. The author, Robert Bazell, is an adjunct professor of Molecular Cellular and Developmental Biology at Yale University. During his career with NBC News as a correspondent, Bazell was one of the first network reporters to cover the emerging AIDS epidemic in the early 1980s.

So, he has a bit of credibility.

Having just dipped my toes in the water, I am humbled and in awe of all the brilliant, committed people connected with developing and testing Herceptin, this drug that holds the promise of saving my life.

"Herceptin" had a prolonged incubation. I suppose you could say.

After the 1976 discovery of oncogenes and the role of genetic alterations in Cancer, groundbreaking research feverishly began. Two researchers at a California-based biotech called Genentech had been successful in cloning several cell growth-regulating genes. Art Levinson and Axel Ullrich were leading this research. Genentech was ardently working to develop medicines for a variety of different diseases. Around the same time, Dr. Dennis Slamon of the UCLA Women's Cancer Research Program, and oncologist Dr. Bill McGuire, from the University of Texas at San Antonio teamed up to understand how and if any of these genes might play a role in cancer. Using "DNA probes," a series of experiments were done to see if any of them might be "over-expressed" in cancer tumors.

One, in particular, stood out. The gene is called HER2.

HER2 instructs cells to form receptors on their surface that send signals telling them to grow and divide, which is part of the standard mechanism that regulates healthy cells. But in some breast cancer tumors, there seemed to be higher than normal levels of the gene. They saw that about a quarter of the breast cancer tumors had an excess of HER2. Now, these cells didn't just have the standard HER2 receptors (about 20K) but up to two million of them, triggering the cancer cells to replicate out of control and the tumors to proliferate. This over-expression eventually became known as "HER2-positive" breast cancer. (Gulp, that's me with the manic "Type A" raging out-of-control cancer cells...)

This discovery led to the development of an "antibody" drug to combat this most virulent and insidious form of breast cancer. For twelve years, Dr. Slamon and his colleagues conducted the laboratory and clinical research that led to the development the new breast cancer drug, Herceptin.

"Herceptin" derived its name from the HER2 genetic over-expression characterizing this aggressive cancer and the "interception" the antibody runs against the "signals" telling the cancer cells to grow and multiply.

The Herceptin antibody project was ridiculed, the funding was pulled and almost shot down many times. While patients in the clinical trials had remarkable responses with the promise of extended lives by years, the board of directors at Genentech were on the verge of shutting the trials down for good based on various political reasons. It appears that credibility with the "GNE" (Genentech's NYSE symbol) board of directors and stockholder pressure were less than benevolent forces. The conscience of medicine was on thin ice, and Herceptin's survival was severely threatened.

So, all is fair in love, war *and cancer* ...when "untold profits" are concerned?

Friday, October 9th
I'm wigging out!

I haven't had a bit of scalp tingle and have not lost a strand of hair. Yet, here I sit in this little number called "Intimate." I look like freaking Florence Henderson in the 70s. This will not do. What I need is a wardrobe of absolutely, positively fabulous hats.

My pending hair loss aside, I'm diving to the bottom of the ocean to try and better understand the relationship between cancer cells and how Herceptin works. When it works, or when it doesn't. Or if and when it stops working.

As I keep reading and re-reading the biology behind all of this, it is beginning to make more sense. Genes are, evidently, like little instruction manuals. They school every cell in our body how to grow, what kind of cell to become, and how to behave. Kind of like, "eat your vegetables, act like a lady, sit up straight, don't slurp your soup, and get good grades." Genes order the cells to make particular proteins that cause a specific activity, like growing, repairing, resting. Some cancer cells have genetic abnormalities that screw up the directions on how much and how fast. Sometimes the cancer cells have too many copies of these abnormal genes. This excess is called "over-expression," which can cause cancer cells to shift into overdrive and make too many proteins that control cell growth and division, causing cancer to grow and spread, as Bazell's book explains. Breast cancer cells that over-express the HER2 gene are said to be HER2-positive.

Herceptin works by attaching itself to the HER2 receptors on the surface of breast cancer cells and blocking them from receiving growth signals. By blocking the signals, Herceptin can slow or stop the growth of breast cancer. In addition to blocking HER2 receptors, Herceptin can also help fight breast cancer by alerting the immune system to destroy cancer cells to which it is attached.

But, from the research I can find, it appears that in some cases, Herceptin is not hugely effective in killing cancer cells – it just delays their growth. The jury seems to be out regarding Herceptin's ability to decrease the activity of its target, the HER2 protein. So, you must have the right amount of over-expression and an immune system like a Ninja Warrior to respond to Herceptin effectively.

Anyway, enough biology for today.

The punch-line confirms what I suspected and feared: the Herceptin antibody is *not* a slam-dunk.

So now I will do my best to refrain from genuinely wigging out.

But, as far as I'm concerned, the ugly wig... can go shag itself.

Tuesday, October 13th
I just returned from San Diego, where we attended a friend's wedding. Brian and I had a wonderful time on the West Coast. Spending time with Jenny, Zach, Kelsey, and Colton in Encinitas was the perfect escape. Nobody talked about "It." It was like we left "It" in Chicago.

I smiled all weekend, keeping my chin up and lipstick freshly applied.

Nobody looked at me with that "You Poor Thing" look. No special treatment. People were rude to me and made a major faux pas, like the woman who sat next to me at the reception who was rambling on about her husband, "the scientist," who does "basic research" for biotech. "Yes, it's interesting to some people, but it's not like he's developing a cure for cancer." (Ha, ha, ha, ha, ha...)

I did corner the Biotech Scientist later in the evening.

I tried prodding him on genetically target therapy, leading him to believe my agency was pitching a "dotcom" focused on mining the internet for patients desperate for cutting-edge clinical trials. (I've learned this is an emerging form of behavioral marketing, as perverse as it seems.) He explained, and I retained just enough to fully appreciate the "Cancer is like a snowflake" analogy. Each patient's diagnosis is unique, and finding a common denominator that ties all these special snowflakes together is the key to developing scalable therapies.

Scalable is key to profits and funding.

The Scientist knew a thing or two about Genentech, a competitor to his employer. When I tried out my analogy describing Herceptin as a "parachute that might open," he smiled. "Bingo," he nodded knowingly as if trading secrets with me.

I immediately aborted my fact-finding mission, grabbed Brian by the arm, and whisked him off to the dance floor, thinking that I might be able to out-fox the Cancer by hiding in the middle of the Chicken Dance.

For the rest of the weekend, I channeled my energy into bonding big time with my little three-and-a-half-year-old niece Kelsey who makes my heart smile and clutching to my dream.

Me, mid-forties. You can tell by the lines around my eyes. I'm standing on a dock in a clear, deep green lake surrounded by trees. The same lake I swam in with my sisters when we were young. It is late summer. The air is filled with laughter and conversation, echoing over the lake. "Aunt Beth, watch me!" Splash. My niece, Kelsey, almost ten years old, makes a perfect swan dive off the deck. "Mommy, watch me..." a small voice says. I look down at my beautiful little daughter, with a smile that could fill the sky and bright blue eyes, just like her Irish father's.

I am filled with greater happiness than I ever imagined.

Catie...

I think we named her Catie.

Wednesday, October 14th

PROJECT: BETH – Status Report:
First, Herceptin infusion, which I will receive bi-weekly

While the jury may be out on how well-matched my HER2 over-expression is to Herceptin's wizardry, I will stick with my guns on being positively optimistic about the drug. If I can be that 0.0000375 that gets HER2+ IBC at age thirty-six, I have a shot at being one of those elite responders.

That said, feeling pleased with this milestone, I completed an assessment of everything that I have accomplished since my diagnosis in August:

Project Beth: QUARTERLY PERFORMANCE REVIEW
- Brian & I were remarried on September 5th
- After thirteen years, I took a break from advertising
- Got my hair cut short to prepare for chemotherapy
- Did not proceed with Northwestern's high-dose plan
- Choose Dr. Cobleigh and her team at Rush Pres. St. Luke's
- Had my first chemotherapy treatment
- Did the "Race for the Cure," posed with survivors for a group photo
- Committed to this Journal, even when the going got rough

Quite a bit accomplished, I'd say. But I am still in the infancy of my treatments, and there is a long road ahead. Seven "big gun" chemotherapy infusions to come. Weekly Herceptin treatments along the way. A mastectomy and lymph node dissection, followed by daily radiation while I receive continued infusions of Herceptin. Reconstruction, if I get that far.

It is too much to contemplate all at once. So, I'll continue to take it one day at a time. And celebrate each one.

> *"Don't let the unchangeable past or the indefinite future steal today."*
>
> *~ Unknown*

And as I get ready to attempt sleep, the first night I've felt I could sleep in six heavy weeks, I visualize a New Sheriff in town, toweringly tall in white chaps and boots with gleaming spurs. And I imagine Herceptin as a "White Drug" coursing through my veins, blinding cancer with benevolence...and I envision the white parachute is unfurling thirty-thousand feet above hard ground.

Thursday, October 15th
I'm molting.

My hair is falling out precisely two weeks and two days following my first chemo-therapy appointment. Just like they said it would.

I've started wearing a hat. It's the only one I have so far, simple and grey, but practical. It arrived from Michigan last week, in a plain cardboard box. No tissue. Not even a card. It felt like a cold and sterile gift. Apropos coming from my family. But on time, nonetheless.

Watching your hair fall out makes the whole cancer-patient thing pretty official. I was looking around the shower in the taxi cab bathroom this morning. My caddy was stocked with shampoos, conditioners, de-tanglers, shaving cream, and razors. And I realized something a tad startling…

All I'll need in the shower is…a bar of soap.

Friday, October 16th, 12:07 pm
I'm trying to make light of it with my soap joke. There is no singing in the shower these days. Not a single note.

The shower has become a scary place I don't want to be.

The hair falling out it clumps all over the tub is one thing, but facing my red can-cer-ridden breast is another. The disease is right there. I can see it. I can feel it. It's not like the invisible monster I've always thought breast cancer to be.

I leave the lights and the fan off so that the dark and the steam obscure insidious cancer living and breeding right under my nose.

It's like "Showering with the Enemy."

The traitor chained to my hem in the light, dark, cold, warm, dry and wet.

I wonder if perhaps I could fake my death...

I could swim the length of Lake Michigan, taking up residence near Door County, Wisconsin, under a new alias. I could waitress at the local diner, attend Friday night fish boils and church every Sunday, dressing plainly and keeping a low profile in some small town where time stands still and the Cancer could never find me.

And every year on the fourth of July, I'd walk to the shore, looking southwest towards Chicago, squint hard, and re-imagine my life before Cancer...

And how sweet freedom felt.

4:08 pm

And as I process all of it, it strikes me how important this writing continues to become for me. I don't know what I would do for companionship without you, my dearest no-name Journal. You are a rudder, a redwood. And ditto for my other best friends, the worn, torn, and water-stained journals.

I have so treasured the escape and listening ear you are providing.

As I've been leafing through Journal One, dressed in its colorful embroidered jacket and blue sewed spine, it makes me smile, and the clouds roll away, at least for this moment, and I bask in the thoughts of a much happier time.

Like that random night in January....

Brian and I were at a little spot called "Sidetracks," enjoying beer and improv comedy. We had been dating for a little over a year. The significant holidays had all passed, and there was nothing to signal that a proposal might be imminent.

Brian proudly put a small box on the table next to a little pool of beer foam.

"Will you?" he asked so sweetly, and in his blue eyes, I could see him envisioning a lifetime of blissful happiness.

How would I have responded if I knew then what I know now?

Perhaps I might have said...." Run, Brian, Run!"

And the Irish Prince would gallop off into the Spanish sunset on a green-speck-led horse with a long red flowing mane, never to be seen or heard from again. But every year on St. Patrick's Day, he would order a round of frothy green beer for all the folks in the town, and they would gather in his pub and have a good long laugh about the silly lass from his past who attracted drama something like the way dust surrounds Pig Pen from Charlie Brown.

And the enchanting Irish Prince lived happily ever after...without me.

This isn't my Hollywood ending. No, not at all.

And I think of all the love lost in the world...and how hard it must have been for Gene Wilder to watch his soulmate Gilda Radner slowly disappear. And all the men who have lost their wives to breast cancer and cancer of any type. Someday this will all be behind me.

And I again imagine the white loons taking graceful flight over infinitely expansive fields of Black Daisies.

Six: Dying But So Full of Life

Saturday, October 17th
Weekends are good for reminiscing.

I'm not feeling incredibly energetic and I'm saving what I got for the next Big Gun chemotherapy production. Lying in wait just around the block. Until then, I'm sneaking away during the intermission, getting further entrenched in Journal One and reliving "The Beginning of Beth and Brian."

In answer to The Question? ... I slept on it.

Literally.

I put that beautiful little ring between my mattress and box spring and slept on it.

When the sun rose the next day, I took a deep breath and decided that, ultimately, I should commit to the person who is my best friend. And on October 14th, 1989, Elizabeth Mary Catherine Distel married Brian Patrick Grady. The guy who made me laugh.

And what a happy day it was when we moved into the Blue House, our first. The grand eighty-year-old American Four-Square on the perfectly tree-lined street. The things I liked best about our Blue House were the gracious front porch, the retro black and yellow tiled "Taxi Cab" bathroom and the vintage dining room chandelier.

The Blue House had plenty of charisma.

Of all the selling points the Blue House had to offer, the one that won my heart was the Old Mulberry Tree in the backyard.

All the renovation we did to make the Blue House our own. We were stripping up the shag carpeting, refinishing the hardwood floors, and giving every room a facelift with a tasteful color palette.

So odd.

We always talked about starting a family, yet the first thing we did to the second bedroom was strip off that Mickey Mouse wallpaper and paint over the blue-sky ceiling with the little white clouds.

I often look back at the photo album that preserves the happy memories of the party we threw in the Blue House that summer. I slaved for weeks planning every detail, Baked polenta and roasted bell pepper dip served with buckets of ice Cerveza and limes on the patio under the Old Mulberry. Colorful conversation and laughter by the liter flowed into the yellow dining room under the vintage chandelier. The wine poured generously between courses of chilled gazpacho with sour cream and scallions, followed by a platter of grilled salmon and swordfish and roasted summer vegetables with balsamic glaze. And for dessert, of course, my signature dish, Margarita Pie, with its wicked kick. Rounds of espresso kept us all laughing into the night back out on the patio for port and cigars. Even the girls.

The best part of the Blue House celebration was unquestionably relaxing under the shade of the Old Mulberry. And she gave a pretty good shade for an old dame.

I've never outwardly admitted this, but I started having conversations with the Old Mulberry Tree sometime after Brian and I moved into the Blue House. I felt the Tree was, in a peculiar way, connected to me.

She had all the "tells" of a wise old soul…and her curious presence was hard to ignore. By the looks of her leathery face and knotted hands, I pegged her pushing near ninety or so (knowing it is always a good idea to underestimate a lady's age). She struck me as spiritually-inclined, and I liked to think she saw the world through birds' eyes, despite being tethered to the ground, as trees by nature are. She sported a thick, noble trunk and dense canopy. Veiled with white and pink blossoms in the spring and verdant and shady in the summer. She cast a long shadow for a petite tree. If a squirrel were to shake one of her limber limbs, her berries would stain the earth with puddles of crimson. She turned out fashionably blazoned in her autumn wardrobe of gold and orange hues few women could pull off so well. But she was at her most magnificent, snow-covered and ice-adorned in the long, cold Chicago winters.

I photographed her every season.

For Brian's birthday that year, I bought him a birdhouse. It was an outhouse, actually, with a crescent moon carved in the door, kitschy but cute. It was, in a way, a gift for the Old Mulberry Tree.

That fall, Brian and I went to Galena to celebrate five years of marriage. We came home to a pile of gold, red, and orange Mulberry leaves covering the walkway. We took pictures with pumpkins, under the Wise Old Mulberry, like two children crouched at their grandmother's feet.

Life was good and we had "it all," it would seem.

"The secret to having it all is believing you already do."

~ Unknown

Could cancer be karma's way of punishing me for having "it all" and throwing it away?

Monday, October 19th
PROJECT: BETH – Status Report:
Second infusion of Adriamycin Cytoxan today.

Dearest Journal, I need to tell you about it while I am feeling well before nausea sets in for a spell.

So, again, the Defective Bride stood in the gateway, surveying the City of Chemopolous. Today, Chemopolous was respectfully quiet, with the requisite muffled coughs and sneezes here and there. I heard a cotton swab being dropped in a room down the hall. The decorative boxes of Kleenex tissues adorning the side tables have been changed from summer themes to autumn. In all her glory, the Queen of Chemopolous held court at the check-in. She sensed my presence, as a perceptive, attentive Queen would naturally do, and tilted her carefully quaffed head to greet me with her tortoise-framed bifocaled glacier blues.

I can almost feel the buzz, buzz, buzz of the soft 30-watt luminescence that the Queen emits, and I look down to see if she might be wearing a pair of stilettos today.

"Elizabeth Grady..." she respectfully greets me without missing a beat. "We were expecting you."

The Queen nods in the direction of station number three, a lovely private spot next to the window, thoughtfully reserved just for me. I'm on the "A-List" today. The Queen raises her perfectly arched eyebrow, searching for a subtle expression of gratitude.

"Thank you for creating a sense of familiarity for me," I manage a polite half-smile.

The Fresh Intern, with eyes as big as saucers, appears again upon cue. She looks like perhaps she has grown an inch or two.

"I like your hat," she offers tentatively as if extending an olive branch in apologies for what will soon follow. "It looks nice on you." I adjust my brown crushed velvet cloche and try to put her at ease. "You know, this one is my favorite," I smile back at her.

She lights up immediately, sensing this will be one of her more straightforward nurse-patient dialogues, "Right this way...."

As we navigate across Chemopolous, I am again keenly aware of "The Eyes" following me as we make our way back to the sunny corner of the room. I am careful to avoid contact with "The Eyes" and let them pretend to be obsessed with their knitting, crocheting and Reader's Digests.

The first time, I clung to the blissful optimism that all those possible side effects might not be relevant to my chemistry, that I might somehow be spared. Round Two is a shade different. I feel myself flush and involuntary flinch. I surrender and reluctantly take a seat in 'The Chair." My right eye is twitching and my neck is in knots. My elbows might be perspiring.

The Fresh Intern puts a tight rubber band around my left arm and again I make a clenched fist. I close my eyes, and a familiar sting surges through the inside of my arm as the catheter is put squarely in place. "First, I'll give you a shot of Benadryl that will make you sleepy and relaxed, and then I will give you..." The Fresh Intern eagerly begins her spiel like a flight attendant narrating the safety video.

I've always thought of safety videos as buzz kills.

My knee-jerk interruption surprises even myself... "I know you are doing the job for which you are paid, but I'm not in the mood for the play-by-play today if that's quite okay. So, if you keep it short, I'll keep it on the QT," and then, to soften the blow, I offer, "But a handful of those lemon drops sounds like the perfect thing." She nods her head ever so slightly as if she does understand but shoots back with a little barb of her own. "We do have a deal if, next time, you can promise to arrive *promptly.*"

As the first wave of drugs starts coursing through my veins, I again fixate on the most distant point on the skyline and vow this time I will not surrender to tears. And before I drift off, I exhale with a deep sigh, imagining the New Sheriff as he rides in with his dazzling smile.

The one side-effect of Herceptin, cognitive heart failure, could threaten to put a kink in the plan. But I'm staying calm and collected. The Universe couldn't possibly be that cruel.

As I hopscotch between Bazell's book on Herceptin and my journals, I decide the latter is bound to be more therapeutic right now. "My Creative Recovery: Continued" fills in the blanks with color, conversations and details I obscured long ago.

As Brian and I settled further in with our intertwined lives, it was clear that I laughed less and less. The words paint a picture of a partnership, more than a marriage, and resentment that I was doing most of the heavy lifting.

Happy-go-lucky Brian played the role of the easy-going creative guy, a copy-writer, and a musician with a fair amount of professional latitude. And comfortable exercising freedom in our personal lives, it seemed. It felt like he spent increasingly more and more time playing with the band and more and more evenings and weekends practicing with the guys. On the other hand, I was busy doing most of the cooking, grocery shopping, and cleaning while managing our finances and trying to plot out a future that would include at least one child at some point.

Around the same time, I felt like a slave in my career. Trapped in the most non-creative department in the agency, crunching numbers and balancing budgets working more and more over time, often late into the night and on weekends. Ironically, I was doing what seemed to me a lot more like accounting than advertising. And I certainly didn't sign up for an exciting career in advertising only to end up counting beans.

I felt like I was making all the sacrifices and compromises.

I didn't particularly appreciate feeling that way.

By the way, Brian and I realized tonight that today would've been our 9th anniversary if you count the hiatus period and add seven days. The anniversary was eclipsed by my first Herceptin treatment last week.

We "celebrated" our forgotten anniversary a week late by exchanging Hallmark cards, eating soy burgers and watching old Seinfeld episodes.

Thursday, October 22nd

Recently parked in the "Quote Book" from one of my favorite authors of all time:

"Everyone is Just waiting."

~Dr.Seuss (of course)

IS everyone 'Just waiting?"

I know I am.

I am waiting for all the hair to fall out already and stop clogging up the shower drain.

Thursday, October 22nd

Dear Journal, I hope you don't mind that I've been gliding off to the Before Cancer Days more often instead of providing status reports with all the medical details. I'm feeling more and more reminiscent, trying to reassemble the pieces of the mutilated puzzle my life became.

And as I am making my way through Journal Two, "My Creative Recovery II," it strikes me that my words got steadily stormy and my penmanship jagged and deliberate.

During this stormy period, I became borderline obsessed with that Old Mulberry Tree. A neighbor noticed that the Old Tree had developed spots on her leaves, a mildew of some sort, we speculated. She was being silently ravaged by something sinister and I felt helpless to save her. I wanted to preserve her beauty before she started to wither away, so I took pictures of her in my final photo shoot of the grand Old Tree that August.

I would tell total strangers about the Old Tree, inexplicably romanticizing her in a poem I wrote that would later become her eulogy:

The Wise Old Mulberry Tree

She bore fruit. She gave shade. She had deep roots.
She was content in one place.
She didn't have to forage or seek water or sun.
The world rolled abundantly at her feet.
unlike the beloved giving tree that generously gave and gave
until she was only a stump
The Mulberry Tree maintained her dignity

*Even on the precipice of death and uncertainty,
she stood magnificently.*

~ Elizabeth M Grady

My poem didn't rhyme very well. But nothing in my life felt like it rhymed at that time.

I showed the photograph to a friend and described the Tree as...." Dying but so full of Life."

"Beth," she said in a prophetic way, "That tree is a *metaphor for you.*"

Friday, October 23rd
I'm spending more time with Bazell's book and doing my cumbersome research online.

I'm trying to piece together an objective account as I am able of what happened with the Herceptin trials and the brave women who paved the way for many other women like me.

For instance, Anne.

When she was diagnosed, Anne was thirty-two, with a husband and a one-year-old son. She had the advantage of some grounding in science, with a biology major and a chemistry minor in college; her first job at Yale Medical School involved testing the effects of chemotherapy on cancer cells. When Anne's self-discovered lump was determined to be malignant as she lay on the operating table, her surgeon performed a radical mastectomy and called it a day. But four years later, Anne found a new lump along her mastectomy scar; tests showed it was malignant. This time her oncologist prescribed chemotherapy, which seemed to keep the cancer in remission for a little over four years when she discovered a second recurrence. Now, her doctor recommended high-dose chemotherapy with bone-marrow rescue, which insurance companies cover to avoid more lawsuits. Before she could begin the high-dose chemotherapy, Anne had to sign a consent form that was more like a death consent. In early 1995, she underwent high-dose chemotherapy the treatment; she noticed two lymph nodes had swollen up again.

Scans showed that cancer had recurred a fourth time.

Anne spent the better part of two decades fighting breast cancer when she finally heard about the treatment that would extend and possibly save her life.

In November 1995, she found an article in The Boston Globe about how patients and doctors turned to the internet to find and recruit for clinical trials. The Globe printed a mention about the HER2/neu trials.

Long story short, Anne entered the protocol offering the Herceptin antibody without chemotherapy, despite the warnings from her doctor, and saw immediate results. Unfortunately, some cancer did recur in May 1997, after she had been on Herceptin for a year.

Anne's last quote in Bazell's book reads with resiliency I can only aspire to.

"My response to it (Herceptin), I think, is just miraculous…I marvel at that…Why me? What does the future hold? Who knows? Discoveries are popping up every day, so maybe something more in the curative line, I'll live to see. I hope."

After twenty years of fighting breast cancer recurrences, Anne stood magnificently.

Just like my Wise Old Mulberry.

Seven: Yes, I'd Choose Cancer Over That

As I reflect on the past two months of writing I have done, it strikes me that some of my most lucid insights have come to me during this medical odyssey.

"Adversity has the effect of eliciting talents, which in prosperous circumstances would have lain dormant."
- Horace (Roman Poet)

"Nothing sharpens the senses and intellect like the prospect of dying"
~ Me

And as I compare and contrast this journal to those of my past, I see such an obvious and definite correlation between my journals and pain.

"The more acute the pain, the more powerful the prose."
~ Also, Me

And on that note, I bravely decided to confront the darkest parts of the warped and stained Journal Two. I need to excise the demons lurking there.

It still makes me ache inside.

I re-read the entry where my friend told me the Old Mulberry Tree was a metaphor for me. She knew I was contemplating leaving behind that chapter of my life, my married life with Brian. In that life, as happy as it may have looked on the surface and as perplexing as my decision would seem to Brian, I felt I was slowly dying. I loved him so much but lost myself in the marriage. The band seemed to occupy more and more of Brian's free time, and the extra bedrooms remained guest rooms with less and less discussion about which one might make the perfect nursery. It became clear that Brian was a creature of habit and was perfectly content with the life we had built just the way it was.

I learned a few things about myself in our almost seven years of marriage.

I knew I had a safe, simple and comfortable life. But being safe and simple wasn't enough.

I remember walking into the counselor's office together, holding hands, and feeling like I was leading a lamb to its slaughter.

I remember sitting together on a large leather sofa in a sparsely furnished office, looking out the window at the cold grey sky.

I remember inhaling and holding my breath.

I remember wincing as the words fell out of my mouth, knowing the pain and destruction they would cause.

"If I believe in life after death, I'd give you this one. But I don't…so I can't."

One of the most horrible and awful things you can ever do is to hurt someone who deeply loves you.

Yes, I'd choose Cancer over that.

But I am no stranger to pain.

My failed marriage and cancer are continuations of the deep wounds I've carried deep within me for decades. But I haven't ever dared to record it in any journals. Exiled memories shivering somewhere in Siberia. The would-be-gardeners swept them that far under the rug. Why is this all coming to the surface now?… Running through my head…again and again… the fluorescent formaldehyde… the black daisies…and the thing at the end of the hall. Haunting music begins to sear through my brain. I can smell the soft autumn rain, as it begins to fall just outside the window, like a whisper against which you are powerless. I open my mouth to warn the Others…danger…the enemy is coming. We have to get out of here. But the Others are deaf. The Others are confined to cribs and have bulbous heads. I can faintly hear his voice reciting a storybook.. Uncle Remus…he read again and again…" and da Tar Bay…*she says nothing…she says NOTHING.*"

Why is all of this running through my brain?

Perhaps this is it…

I've finally gone insane.

> *"There are two types of pain;*
> *one that hurts you*
> *and*
> *one that changes you."*
>
> - Unknown

Sunday, October 25th

I decided I needed to get out of the house.

For something other than a doctor's appointment.

I bravely headed to Michigan Avenue to buy myself a few hats, which I'm in desperate need of.

I found my way to the millinery department at Marshall Fields in the Water Tower. As I was standing in the three-way mirror trying on different styles, I realized my quickly-thinning hair was now falling out in huge clumps if I ran my hands through it, scratched my head, or put a hat on and took it off.

As I stood in the department store with hair-locks on my lapels and at my feet, I became aware of a small child staring at me. Then I noticed the mother pulling him away and informing a skinny sales associate that there was an "uncomfortable situation" she needed to attend to. The skinny sales associate suggested I go into a private dressing room so I wouldn't "upset the other customers." And, for that matter, perhaps I should come back another time "After the hair loss was over." The skinny sales associate kept nodding like a bobble head as if to amplify what an excellent recommendation she was making.

Instead, she made me feel like a freak show.

But I decided I would not be intimidated and was not leaving that quickly. Not without a fabulous hat. I told the skinny head-nodding sales associate. "I'll take this navy blue one, please. And I'll take my future business to Lord & Taylor so you can close my charge account here." And then, for other punctuation, "And, in the event, you don't know anyone who has gone through chemotherapy, losing all your hair is an awful experience. Thank you for your compassion."

I picked up my hair from the floor, stuffed it in my trench coat pocket and left the store in a dignified huff, wearing my new navy-blue hat with the extra wide brim, feeling F#@$ing fabulous.

7:13 pm

Feeling just a tad superficial that all I did was buy a hat and admonish a skinny salesperson today, I decided to nestle down with "HER2" and immerse myself further into the trials and tribulations of the making and testing of the drug.

One of the most challenging parts of the journey for Dr. Slamon, and the more emotionally engaged clinicians in the trials, must have been selecting and denying women for participation in the clinical trials.

The initial women were selected for Phase One based on having metastatic HER2-positive breast cancer to see if an antibody developed in mice and humanized would produce any adverse reaction. I don't think any of them expected Herceptin would save their lives. Most of them were worn down by chemotherapy and at the end of their line. But, many of them saw terrific results, tumors shrinking and pain subsiding. They could eat and walk and felt almost good again.

They celebrated holidays and birthdays their doctors had told them they wouldn't.

And then, for the following phases, they couldn't keep all of them—no provision allowed for compassionate use outside of a clinical trial. The patients and their families begged for their lives. Many of them became heroes in the name of medical research so that the test could be completed and other women could live.

If Herceptin does prove to be a miracle drug for me, how could I ever honor them and their families?

Perhaps the Universe will show me a way.

Monday, October 26th

PROJECT: BETH – Status Report:
- Herceptin number two today.
- Had a standard echocardiogram, congestive heart failure has proven not to be a threat.
- Upon inspection of my breast, Dr. Cobleigh thought the skin looked more normal, and the tumor appeared to be "melting."

This notion of the tumor "melting" away is a positively beautiful thought. But, considering the negative mammogram and regular breast exam before my diagnosis, it is hard for me to trust anything right now.

One thing is for sure; I'm glad I can pay a professional to look at my poor red breast because I have not been able to since the nipple turned in. It is like we are life-long friends who are no longer on speaking terms.

On a different note, the time I spend sitting in the waiting room of the oncology department has been an event in itself.

Today, I met Judy.

Judy has had three different types of cancer: Breast, her first. Ovarian, her second. And now melanoma.

Judy dismisses the latest bout with carcinoma as "...just a house fly, really, Dear." It seemingly is, given that her husband passed away last year just before their 50th anniversary of an aggressive form of throat cancer. The doctors rearranged and dismantled the poor man's face until he was unrecognizable.

Judy is taking tango lessons at age seventy-two.

"Leroy wouldn't want me to be sitting at home being a wallflower," she told me... "When I'm out on the dance floor, I feel him there watching me whirl and twirl, and it's like we are young again...like the day I first laid eyes on him, so handsome in his navy uniform."

"You must miss Leroy terribly," I wished I had a more eloquent response.

"Oh my, dear...Love doesn't go to the grave...he is with me every day," Judy smiled with conviction as if Leroy was sitting right there in the seat beside her in the oncology waiting room, looking positively dashing in his navy-blue uniform, complete with spit-shined shoes and spats, his hat properly resting in his lap.

Tuesday, October 27th
Last night, I had one of those moments I have been prone to recently, where I feel like I am peering into someone else's life, and this is some bizarre, twisted reality TV show. After all, how could this possibly be real?

I was standing in the faux-finished rag-rolled blue bedroom. The lights were off but the moonlight filtered in from the skylights. I pulled off the little grey cap I'd been wearing since the last locks of my hair had thinned away. I studied the strange girl looking back at me.

She had just one lock of hair dangling delicately on her head's right side.

"Who have you become?" I whispered to the strange balding girl. She blinked back at me. Then I tugged at the last strand of hair, which surrendered and laid lifeless in my hand.

This morning I tied a ribbon around the last lock of brownish-blond hair and put it in a plastic bag. I remember my mother used to save our locks when we were babies and got our "first haircut." They were lovingly preserved in our little pink baby books, with dates and photos of first birthday cake, first steps, first words, and other not-to-be-forgotten "firsts."

Well, I know my first haircut was precisely documented, and pretty sure Jennifer's was too. Catherine's is probably a crap shoot, and Amy, I doubt she even got a baby book. There is very little public evidence that my youngest sister had an actual childhood. My mother, who had a full plate with four preschoolers by the time she was just twenty-three, kept recycling baby pictures of Catherine, telling everyone they were Amy's. And everyone bought it.

That is how things go for those lower on the birth order totem pole.

I stowed my "Major Haircut" ribbon-tied lock in the plastic sandwich bag in my "Secret Drawer" for safekeeping.

Now, it's not at all what you are thinking. A secret drawer is not a place for things you don't want your mother-in-law to see. It is someplace no one else knows about and wouldn't dare to go.

I sorted through my tangled web of emotions, sealed off like Pandora's Box.

The gold engraved "I Love You" bracelet. Presented to me at age thirteen by my first true love shortly after we celebrated our Catholic Confirmations and subsequently sacrificed our virginity to one another in a patch of pine trees. Underneath that souvenir lies photos of Marina Del Ray that I took on my last day in the Vortex. I was so miserable in LA that I barely noticed the paradise that was my temporary home for two years. Various ticket stubs from my first dates with Brian and pages from my date book that had significance only he would understand. A lifetime of private heartbreak and life lessons kept carefully pre-served and hidden from sight.

I said a silent prayer to the Universe as I laid my locks on the pile of memorabilia and pictured myself ten years from now, with long hair, opening the drawer and remembering the day the last strands of my hair fell out.

And then it occurred to me... It was high time to take a break from those damn Clairol hot rollers, anyway.

Wednesday, October 28th

If I didn't know I had cancer, today could be like any other. So, why shouldn't I be happy today? Aside from a part of my body that is "sick," the rest of me is working just fine.

And on that "happy" note, I am asking the Universe for the opportunity to tackle "Project: Beth Phase II." Which includes some vital "to-dos."

Ring in the new millennium. Hug old classmates at my 20th Class reunion. Train for and run a marathon. Or two. See more of the world. Sit in a café in Paris sipping Bordeaux in the middle of the day, watching the world go by. Float on a barge down the Rhine River. Stand among the Coliseum ruins in Rome and contemplate the universe's enormity, everything that has come before me, and everything that will follow. Visit the Vatican and marvel at how much time the Impressionists had on their hands. Make the Guards at Buckingham laugh. While in London, walk through Parks instead of around them. Do fundraising for Gilda's Club and Y-Me. Celebrate my 40th birthday. Buy a convertible. Drive-up Pacific Coast Highway. Turn this journal into a book. Present it as a THANK YOU gift. Do the 3-Day Walk and be the first survivor to finish. Take a helicopter over a glacier.

And, if the outlook for my longer-term survival looks promising, I'll get a dog.

A terribly adorable dog that I will spoil rotten.

Thursday, October 29th

Dear Journal, still feeling a bit blue? Yes, me too. I've spent more time with that heavy Journal number two. No wonder the cover is all stained and warped.

It was an uncontested divorce.

I remember the judge firing all of these questions in rapid succession....

Were you married in Lake County on October 14th, 1989? ... Yes. Have you been previously separated? ...Yes. Have irreconcilable differences arisen? Yes. Was there an irretrievable breakdown of the marriage? Yes. I remember openly crying in court through the entire series of questions, and as the gavel came down with a deafening thud, I saw a guillotine in my mind's eye. I killed it. My marriage was officially dead.

A week later, a large moving truck pulled up in front of The Blue House on the perfect, shady tree-lined street. Slowly and deliberately, the life we had built together and worked so hard at making together, piece by piece, began to be dismantled in the same manner.

Before I showed myself to the door for good, I put helpful notes everywhere I could. Like post-it notes in the cookbooks, reminding Brian what the best recipes were. As if making a Margarita Pie someday would alleviate his loneliness and pain. Then I left him a message on the answering machine, so he could hear my voice if he needed to. I broke down toward the end of the recording. Please forgive me. Someday maybe you will understand. I shut the door and looked back in from the outside. I no longer lived there.

I think I heard the Blue House sigh sadly and the Old Mulberry shed a few leaves.

Brian called me a couple of days after I moved out of the Blue House. "The Mulberry Tree fell last night."

On a perfectly still night in September, the Old Mulberry Tree gently laid down on her side, taking care not to crush anything in her path. It was as if she decided to pass away peacefully in her sleep.

My friend, who saw the tree as a metaphor for me, bought me a gift shortly after: A small tree covered with bright, young leaves.

It was the very sad end of my marriage and the Old Mulberry.

But, possibly, a new beginning for me.

Eight: Dancing in the Rain

Saturday, October 31st
Dear Journal... Boo!

A letter from my father arrived today, which is rare as Inflammatory Breast Cancer. As I've warned you, our family seems to communicate without actually communicating. And my father, complex as he is, sets the pace. In an uncharacteristic admission of self-awareness, he once jokingly referred to himself as the "Great Communicator."

I'm not sure what he was trying to say in the letter, the words written with such controlled and sharp precision penmanship, befitting an accountant. The letter was haunting. I repeatedly re-read the only letter my father sent me, trying to decipher what felt like an act of contrition.

(Pause)

To celebrate this sinister holiday, Brian and I rented "Scream-2" and passed out treats. Brian donned an unruly wig (not mine) and a baseball cap and proclaimed himself "Otto the bus driver, you know, from "The Simpson's." The kids loved it.

We stayed up "late" and watched Saturday late-night TV. A commercial for Propecia came on: "Are you afraid of losing more hair?" Sitting there bald as Michael Jordan, I spontaneously and honestly yelled, "No!" Brian and I laughed so hard we both cried.

So today, a TV commercial for an anti-balding drug moved me to tears.

Monday, November 2nd
A Letter to My Grandmother Virginia...

Dear Grandmother,

It is almost as if someone throws the switch here in Chicago. It's 75 degrees and sunny...Indian summer...then you are suddenly wearing wool! But I am not complaining. I love autumn.

My schedule is a bit more "relaxed" than it has been in 13 years. And that's o.k. Tuesday is "Museum Day." Wednesday and Thursday are "Volunteer Days." I work at Y-Me, a national Breast Center Organization as a volunteer in their development group. I have also joined a support group at "Gilda's Club." Gene Wilder started this organization in memory of his late wife, who lost her battle with cancer, the comedian Gilda Radner. (Remember? It's always something!) "The Club," as I call it, is a beautiful haven. And on Fridays, I visit BBDO. So that they don't forget who I am.

I made the semi-national news this past weekend. WGN-TV interviewed me at the "Walk for Hope" on Sunday. There I was...looking bald but smiling the whole time.

Brian & I are making the sojourn to Michigan for Christmas and your 89th Birthday. I hope you recognize me!

I think of you often, and I hope your vision stays sharp so you can enjoy your books.

All My Love and Carpe Diem.

~ Elizabeth

Tuesday, November 3rd
In addition to Gilda's Club and my volunteering, I've begun attending a "Young Women's Support Group" for women under 40 with breast cancer. It is inspirational to see all these intelligent and otherwise healthy young women going through breast cancer with so much courage and grace, all in their 20s and 30s. This disease seems to hand-pick the most amazing women.

One girl is just twenty-two.

I haven't made a habit of complaining through this whole ordeal, but it strikes me as so incredibly unjust and unfair. We should be thinking about diapers and daycare.

Not disability and dying.

Usually, when I tell people I have Inflammatory Breast Cancer, they get that "Ooooooh" look on their faces. Not with this group. When I told them I had IBC, one of the ladies said, "Wait until you meet Shannon!"

Shannon is an Inflammatory Breast Cancer survivor. She is my age and also career-oriented. From what I understand, she is a successful pharmaceutical sales rep. She has been out of treatment for six months and is celebrating by traveling through Europe. Her blond hair is growing back and she looks radiant in front of the Eiffel Tower, in the picture they gave me. I will meet Shannon next week. I can't wait. I suspect that Shannon and I will become fast friends.

By the way, I received a card from a twenty-year breast cancer survivor today. On the front, a lone ballet dancer and the caption: "Those who hear not the music think the dancer is mad."

She signed it, "Beth, LISTEN to the music."

So, today I listened to music. Classical music. Henryk Górecki's powerful "Symphony of Sorrowful Songs." And today, the deep and stirring classical music moved me to tears.

Friday, November 6th
PROJECT: BETH - Status Report:
The entire day was spent on questionnaires for my insurance company.

I started feeling sorry for myself for having to fight for insurance coverage for the incredibly expensive Herceptin, which could be almost $100,000 for the entire course of treatments. Then I gave myself a swift kick in the behind and started thinking of all the courageous women in the Herceptin clinical trials and that their ultimate sacrifice may benefit me. And I was also thinking about the women who leveraged their connections to get the Herceptin trials funded.

According to Bazell's book, after the roller-coaster of events threatening to shut down the trials and funding for Herceptin, Dr. Dennis Slamon was eventually able to complete the tests due to generous donations from the Revlon Foundation and the Entertainment Industry Foundation. The EIF grant was secured through influence wielded by an impressive lady named Lisa Paulsen and Revlon's donation due to connections made by an equally remarkable lady named Lillian. Lillian was the wife of the late Brandon Tartikoff, a media mogul and head of NBC who was a longtime cancer fighter.

Someone should turn Lillian's and Brandon's story into a screenplay.

The daughter of Holocaust survivors, Lillian, attended public schools while growing up in Los Angeles. At a young age, she received a scholarship to study ballet at The David Lichine and Irina Kosmovska Ballet School. She danced her way onto the New York City Ballet company and performed on stages worldwide, including Russia, Germany, Denmark, London and Paris.

In 1982, Lilly married Brandon, and they had two daughters, Calla and Elizabeth. Brandon's battle with Hodgkin's began at age twenty-three and was extremely long, exhausting his medical options in August last year. At the age of forty-eight.

Lillian defined grace and courage during and after her husband's fatal illness. She has channeled her loss into her crusade for a cure, wielding her influence and connections to benefit fundraising for cancer research. Eight years ago, along with Ronald Perelman, CEO of Revlon, she helped create the Revlon/UCLA Women's Cancer Research Program under Dr. Dennis Slamon. The Fire & Ice Ball was also established in Hollywood that year to raise funds for this program to advance clinical trials more quickly, which helped Herceptin progress to the FDA for approval.

I think about that lone ballet dancer on the card the twenty-year survivor sent me, and I imagine cold rain pouring down on her... but the dancer doesn't stop to seek shelter. She holds her head high, faces the sky, and keeps her line and balance while executing developpes, pirouettes, and arabesques with perfection and grace.

Just like Lillian.

Monday, November 9th

PROJECT: BETH - Status Report:
- Today was my 3rd Adriamycin Cytoxan infusion
- My white blood cell count is beginning to teeter
- I will begin daily self-administered shots of Neupogen.
- 3rd Herceptin infusion
- Cobleigh remarked that my tumor continues to "melt" and a "funky" lymph node has gone away

"This is terrific, "she said.

As an act of Carpe Diem, I planted a hundred red tulip bulbs in the backyard before my chemotherapy this morning. I've heard it said, when you plant things it shows you believe in tomorrow. So, a hundred beautiful red tulips, all lie dormant in my backyard.

As distant as it may seem, I believe spring is waiting for me.

Wednesday, November 12th

New friends are coming out of the woodwork, it seems. Her name is Maria. She is from Casablanca, Morocco. We were introduced at Gilda's Club because of our same age and similar diagnosis. She is being treated for breast cancer here in Chicago, speaks little English, and needs some companionship. She is separated from her young son and husband while she lives with her sister in a high-rise.

As daunting as my own experience has been, I cannot fathom being in a different country and culture and relying on others to translate for you.

I will try the museums on Tuesdays with Maria and see how it goes. I hope to bring some joy into what must be a dark, lonely and frightening time for her.

Who knows? Maybe I'll be visiting her in Casablanca someday.

Thursday, November 13th

Si Dieu le veut.

"God Willing," in French.

When I told her my plans to go to Paris when my treatments were finished, Maria reminded me that God would decide if I went.

We went to Shedd Aquarium together. We had lunch together. We talked about religion, our husbands, our families, having children and how breast cancer changes those plans. I know more about Maria than other friends I have known for many years.

We talked about things we could do together. We decided we could exercise together. She has a health club in her building, with a swimming pool. I offered to take her to my club for a change of scenery.

She would like a wig but cannot afford one. I promised Maria I would help her find the perfect wig and take her to the Wig Bank at Y-Me next week. She smiled gratefully at me with her big brown eyes and said, "Thank You, Beth," with such sincerity I will never forget it.

I told Maria I'd be happy to help her with her English and interpreting for medical results, although, fortunately, her sister works for Northwestern. Hence, she has some familiarity with the healthcare system. In return, Maria said she would help me pick up some French. I'm excited about this because I intend to put it to use when I visit Paris for my first cancer anniversary. Si Dieu le veut, of course.

I asked the Universe to show me how to pray.

It sent me Maria.

Monday, November 30th
PROJECT: BETH – Status Report:
- 4th round of chemotherapy.
- Completed the Adriamycin, the most toxic drug I will receive.
- I've had chronic nose-bleeds; the nurse will notify Cobleigh.

This is where I've heard you discover the door in your floor. After treatment number four.

Did I tell you why they call Adriamycin the "Red Devil?" They ask you to flush the toilet three times after you start eliminating it. I've read about children and the elderly dying from "The Red Devil." It is that toxic. If that doesn't scare the crap out of you, I don't know what will. I can't think about what the poison is doing to my poor, ravaged body once the chemical is released into my bloodstream.

Really, in this day and age, is this the best drug we can produce to fight this disease? My temper is starting to rise.

Or is that the hot flushes I've started having?

Monday, December 7th
Thirty-Seven.

Never in my wildest imagination did I think I'd be celebrating it with a bald head and getting intravenous drugs.

> **"Age is just a number of how many winters you've seen.**
> **It says nothing about how cold the winters were."**
>
> *K. Roberta*

Wednesday, December 9th
In my Y-Me Young Women's Group tonight, I finally met Shannon. She is the first IBC survivor I have met since my diagnosis.

They aren't many of us.

Shannon is from a Midwestern family, like me. She is athletic, like me. She financed her college education and went to grad school, like me. She even shops at Ann Taylor, like me. Shannon is, in fact, a lot like me.

The group talked about our lifestyles and what could have caused our breast cancer at such a young age. One lady is a vegetarian. Another is a fantastic tennis player. A majority of them never smoked. And only a few used oral contraception. Some of the women have children. One of the women was diagnosed while pregnant and had to wait several months until the baby was born to receive chemotherapy. Not at all the older, post-menopausal, overweight and inactive stereotype I had always heard about.

Did we do something to bring this on ourselves? We all wonder.

I think to myself, perhaps this is how years of Catholic Guilt ultimately manifest themselves.

Saturday, December 12th
Shannon and I went out for a light dinner and champagne last night. A belated birthday celebration of sorts. She chose someplace special where we would get a lovely private table with the best sommelier in the city.

The perfect excuse to wear the newest fabulous hat in my expanding collection; crimson with a vintage, crushed appearance, as if I have been wearing it for years.

Over oysters and champagne, I tell Shannon that I will write a memoir about my "medical odyssey" if I make it to my fifth anniversary. I told her it was a promise I had made to myself and that I had a special dedication in mind. My book would be written from the perspective of an empowered self-advocate, not blindly accepting standard protocol. I would encourage women to research and participate in treatment decisions. Access to more health and medical information through the internet will radically change the way patients will behave, I predicted. I want my book to encourage that. But, my book wouldn't be cliche or jammed pack with every minute medical detail. It would be a genuine, sensitive and beautiful tale with a liberal dose of my sarcastic humor.

Shannon agreed wholeheartedly with my thoughts on tonality and has been working on a memoir about the positive aspects of breast cancer and how cancer has given her new life. It's mostly a collection of short stories, and she is thinking about how to weave them together.

Shannon's life "B.C." was picture perfect, at least on the surface. She had a traditional Midwestern upbringing, was a competitive tennis player in high school and also one of the best in her class in track, graduating top of her class from Notre Dame, followed by a nursing career, marriage to a successful real estate developer, a beautiful home and an active social life with a large circle of friends.

All of that...and did I mention she can stop traffic? Shannon is one of the most stunningly beautiful women I've known. Shannon had it "all."

Then the life-altering phone call from her doctor. The surgery, the chemotherapy, followed by a divorce from a superficial husband who couldn't handle her diagnosis, infertile and now imperfect body. The bitter divorce that cost her a home and many "friends."

Even her dog.

"I heard the most beautiful quote the other day," Shannon told me, pausing intently, freezing that particular moment in time, then stretching it back like a slingshot and exhaling with:

"I just want to live until I die."

With frightened but intense eyes, she leaned in close and whispered, "Beth, my doctor thinks I may have a recurrence."

Everything stopped.

For a full thirty seconds, I think.

The waiters, the other guests, the champagne fizz, my breathing...time stood still as if we were stuck in a freeze frame of a Diner's Club commercial. I sat staring into her steely blue eyes, terrified to blink. When I finally exhaled, the spell was broken. "I'll be by your side," I blurted out awkwardly, unprepared for this holiday present.

"I'm taking it one step at a time," Shannon said calmly. "But, tonight, we are smart and strong and ready to take on the town. I think that calls for more champagne." And then she smiled with an arched eyebrow .... *"And dancing!"*

True to my word, I was by Shannon's side every step, including every club where she wanted to "be seen." The seemingly infinite night will forever remain a mélange of VIP entrances, secret rooms with blue lights, and effervescence in long-stemmed flutes in an underground universe that seemed to comprehend, Carpe Diem very much includes seizing the night.

We danced like our lives depended upon dancing. We danced until we could no longer feel our swollen, bleeding feet. We danced like it was our last night on earth. And walked home barefoot, as the sun was coming up.

> *"Life isn't about waiting for the storm to pass.*
> *It's learning to dance in the rain."*

— Unknown

As the morning light fills the Blue House, I sit at my pine desk in last night's clothes with the faint smell of fine champagne lingering on my breath. I know it is not my responsibility to save Shannon from what lies ahead.

I *can't* save Shannon.

But I can honor her by living every day without the promise of tomorrow.

A philosophy that will be *certain* to soil my reputation.

If I keep this up.

Nine: Tits in Your Shoes

Monday, December 14th

We Distel women are not easily kept down. I'm often reminded that it is in our lineage by my dear Grandmother Virginia.

My grandmother is an interesting woman.

She is beyond worldly, yet she has never been outside of the U.S.; never traveled beyond the borders of Michigan and Ohio, as far as I know. She is a traditionalist who defied societal conventions. She has a broad circle of friends and loves good conversation and family gatherings, yet she has lived like a lone wolf in many respects. She has an exquisite taste for art and the finer things in life, yet she came from and was returned to a life of very modest means. I feel an inextricably strong connection to her, yet we rarely speak. She is a breathing bundle of self-contradictions.

My grandmother was and will always be, even in her slower years: A paradox.

In a way, that is the most dependable part about her.

Virginia Mitchell, or Ginny, as her close friends call her, has been described as a "handsome" woman in her earlier days. Stately. Sturdy. Always impeccably turned out. "You can tell a well-dressed woman by her shoes and handbag," she has always said. And Ginny was always well-heeled and carrying something so well made it didn't require a logo or a designer label. Her sense of style and taste for the elegant was instinctual, having grown up in a poor neighborhood in Cincinnati. To this day, she is ashamed of the near-poverty living conditions that defined her upbringing, including the awful bedbugs, and rarely speaks of her childhood.

The one part of her "roots" she proudly embraces is her Irish heritage.

Ginny managed to crawl out of the Ohio Irish-Catholic ghetto and moved to Detroit, where she married pretty well. She wed a handsome and successful first-generation German gentleman named Ferdinand Isadora Distel and became one of Motor City's socialites back in the halcyon days of the auto industry. Ginny made certain her large home on Breton Drive was decorated with great style and unique art pieces. She had a penchant for owls and over a hundred as paintings, statues, needlepoint, paperweights and other assorted knick-knacks honoring the wise birds. Ginny also had a gift for the art of conversation and entertainment. Ginny and "Freddy" hosted many a party in their lovely home. They were famously known for their Sunday afternoon ice cream socials during summer months. Ginny was the consummate hostess, ensuring all of her guests were well-attended to and encouraged the ladies to linger into the dusk hours, relaxing on the veranda.

Now, my grandmother can spin a tale better than most, but, more importantly, she is an attentive listener. Back then, she was adept at drawing out the most interesting stories from her guests by hardly talking about herself. The less she spoke, the more she heard.

"Everyone has a story to tell," she still reminds me to this day.

When the children were old enough to sit for long periods, Ginny commissioned an emerging artist to do portraits of her family, including three children, Danford Daniel, Terrence Joseph and dear Gretchen.

Gretchen's birth was a test of Ginny's strength. The doctors made a mistake in the delivery, using forceps that left Gretchen with brain damage. Gretchen developed just enough to understand she was developmentally disabled, which broke Ginny's heart. She made every effort to protect Gretchen. However, her sons weren't quite as sensitive and would torment their poor sister every chance they could. I remember the grainy black and white home movies with my father and uncle beckoning to her," Fly, Gretchen, Fly!" and young Gretchen would flap her arms like a little bird, weaving across the expansive, manicured lawn, trying with all of her might to take flight.

Aside from the special care her daughter required, Ginny had managed to cultivate a very civilized and privileged life.

The love of her life, Freddie, ran the travel bureau at the iconic Cadillac Book Hotel in the heart of what was then a vibrant throbbing downtown Detroit. Freddie was well-connected and well-liked by his affluent clientele, including Hollywood stars, politicians and international automotive executives. He was known to occasionally secure companionship in addition to travel accommodations with the assistance of his sister Mary who ran the most respectable brothel in all of Motor City. Halcyon days, indeed.

Ginny's story took an unexpected and tragic turn when, at the relatively young age of fifty-two, Freddie suffered a fatal heart attack. The enormous loss was amplified when, amidst her mourning, Ginny was informed by their accountant that Frederick did not have his financial house in order. As opulent as their life-style appeared on the surface, Frederick had not invested, saved, or ensured anything, including his own life.

Ginny was left a widow without means and soon moved out of the elegant home into a modest flat where she could barely make ends meet. Like that, Ginny Mitchell-Distel was as poor as a Cincinnati church mouse.

Ginny found herself waiting on the women she once entertained in her elegant home, selling shoes, handbags and clothing she could no longer afford at a department store in Birmingham. But, soon enough, Ginny's eye for style and the art of conversation secured her a loyal following of customers. Eventually, she became the store's lead bridal consultant, much in demand. Ginny became a self-sufficient single mother, proudly defying societal conventions at that time. But Ginny was, as it became evident, far from conventional. She turned down several suitors, as Frederick only and only great love, and not to be replaced for financial security or social acceptance.

But, eventually, Ginny did marry again.

It depends on which family member you ask, but the story of how Ginny met her husband number two goes something like this...

On one particular St. Patrick's Day, sometime in the late 1950s, as a woman proud of her Irish heritage, Ginny, took to a stool in a proper Irish pub in Birmingham for a plate of corned beef and cabbage and a pint of green beer. The next part of the story has been presented to me over the years with different nuances, depend-ing on which Distel was telling the tale. Still, I often defer to my sister Catherine's account, which is the closest approximation of the truth, I believe...

(Pause) Ah, the phone is ringing.

PROJECT: BETH - Status Report:
- Rush-Pres called to confirm my 2p ENT appointment.
- 11 Scoping II my sinuses due to chronic nose bleeding.

I didn't want to mention it earlier. I don't mean to sound cynical, but if I have a tumor growing in my sinuses, I promise to look fondly back on these good old days when I was so blessed to only have breast cancer.

Tuesday, December 15th

Project: Beth – Status Report:

The ENT wasn't allowed to share the result with me, but when I melted into a pool of holiday tears, he assured me they saw nothing suspicious.

Enough already with all the cancer nonsense.

Now, where were we?

Oh my! I left poor Ginny alone on a stool at the proper Irish pub on St. Patrick's Day.

So, Ginny sits in her fashionable heels and fine handbag, which caught the eye of a pretty stylish man. A German gentleman, by the name of Harold. "May I join you at the bar?" the handsome, well-appointed younger man politely inquired. Ginny looked Harold up and down and responded flatly, "Well, I don't see why not. Anyone can sit at the bar." And the rest is history.

Although my grandmother and Harold did marry, it was purely for companionship and fashion advice. They maintained separate sleeping quarters, which I never entirely understood as a child. Just as I was baffled when my father used to remark that Harold was "a little light in his loafers." Sort of a Kennedy-Monroe era equivalent of "Will & Grace."

The unsinkable, unconventional Virginia Mitchell-Distel-Schoenborn. I'll do her proud.

Wednesday, December 16th

Dear Journal, everything happens for a reason. They say that is true. Is that what you would say if this all happened to you?

They also say time and distance have the power to heal. And so begins Journal Three, "Journey of a Soul."

A very lost soul.

After the divorce, I ended up on the west coast, where my Anne Taylor wardrobe and Clairol electric hot rollers didn't fit in.

Los Angeles.

Great position with McCann LA, overseeing one of their cornerstone accounts in a sleek office with a view of the foothills and the Hollywood sign. I could see from the Pacific Ocean to San Bernardino. The "Tower of Power" we referred to the building situated in Mid-Wilshire on the fringe of Beverly Hills.

Lovely apartment in Marina Del Ray with a romantic little view of the Pacific Ocean, Playa Del Ray, and at night, the taillights of the planes gliding into LAX. The ocean breeze filled the apartment, and I could almost hear the waves at night. I would strap on my Rollerblades and blade through Venice Beach, Santa Monica, and up to Malibu and back several times a week. The best physical shape I've been in my life.

It doesn't sound too bad, you might say. But home to the celebrity elite and all things beautiful was dubbed "The Vortex" by me.

After I decided to leave Chicago, Brian proclaimed he would never love again and, instead, would become the world's best guitarist. I think he meant it. He threw himself deeper into his music and eventually wrote a song for me.

A parting gift, if you will.

"I like things the way they are; she keeps wishing on a star…
She got me. She got me."

Sometime later, I was leafing through an industry magazine, and I came upon some pictures of an award ceremony in Chicago, and there he was. I was startled by how much he had changed in less than a year. His face, once round, was gaunt, and his eyes, once animated and sparkling, were vacant and distant like a ceramic statue of a lesser-known saint. He had started wearing glasses which overwhelmed his face. He was dressed in a suit I had bought him for our rehearsal dinner, which now engulfs his thinner frame. He was forcing a smile that may have fooled those who knew him less. Underneath that manufactured magazine smile, I saw something that scared me.

Something was very wrong.

I soon forgot how to laugh entirely in L.A.

In the evenings, I would sit on my balcony overlooking the Pacific Ocean, rocking myself repeatedly, listening to Ralph Covert's "Cold, Cold Shivers" over and over and over, feeling confused, worried, and alone. "…We were helpless once our choice had been made, like a bullet in a barrel of a gun that had been fired…." The words kept hitting me, like seaweed being washed ashore after a storm.

Was this how a "new beginning" is supposed to feel?

Saturday, December 19th
Cancer cards, phone calls and letters have stopped coming.

Of course, everyone is busy with family, travel, shopping, baking and entertaining friends and family…no time for consoling sick friends. Heavens, who wants to be bothered with cancer during the holidays? Indeed, not me!

That's the most challenging part of cancer. The loneliness of it. The realization that the world is going on without you.

Monday, December 21st
PROJECT: BETH - Status Report
5th Chemotherapy (1st Taxol) and 6th Herceptin infusion.

I visualized the White Drug, coursing through my veins with its blinding benevolence.

Ho, ho, ho.

Tuesday, December 22nd
Today I woke up MAD.

I thought the stages of grief were denial, anger, bargaining, depression and acceptance. In that particular order. But I began with negotiation, then moved on to denial for three whole days waiting for the pathology. I have been hovering between a mild state of acceptance and a calm state of melancholy for the past two and a half months. It's like I skipped the second phase altogether.

But here it is. Anger, showing up to the party fashionably late and just in time for the holidays.

And as I re-process all that has been inflicted on me and the poison, slashing and burning ahead of me, I get more incensed. Not a controlled anger that I can channel into anything constructive, but certifiably dark and raging MAD.

I honestly thought I would never be so weak as to loathe in self-pity and wonder, "why the hell me?" But you know what, Dear Journal, I don't know why I was plucked out of the crowd to get this vicious form of breast cancer at a relatively young age and lose so much. My hair, my breast, the hope of having children, possibly my advertising career, friends who have disappeared into the woodwork, my sexuality.

I feel naked and flogged. It's like I'm fading away a little bit more every day. What will be left of me in four months? Will Brian still want to claim my damaged goods? Even if I live, what is our prognosis for a normal, happy future?

Adversity is like a strong wind.
It tears away from us all but the things that cannot be torn,
So that we see ourselves as we are."

~ *Arthur Golden*

"It's only after we've lost everything that we're free to do anything."

~ Chuck Palahniuk

I don't know Arthur and Chuck. That sounds like a support group mantra for the homeless.

Monday, December 28th

PROJECT: BETH – Status Report
- Receive my 7th infusion of Herceptin.
- First, Taxol, which is less toxic than Adriamycin.

My lungs are raspy, my nose is bleeding, and the chemotherapy has caused a severe acne breakout. And I have hot flashes.

It is "official."

I am in peri-menopause at age thirty-seven, of all the things to be early for. The fact that I will never be able to have children is a loss I can barely begin to mourn. And to top that off, I think how raving insane it is that I have to deal with acne and hot flashes simultaneously. This makes me MAD too.

I came home and burrowed under the bed covers where I thought I might stay until this damn year was over. But I eventually found the strength to put one toe on the floor, and then my whole foot…and coaxed myself downstairs and into boiling water for green tea. After three McCann LA mugs and a few rounds of a tear-provoking violin rendition of "The Ashokan Farewell," I finally pulled my head out of my ass and put on a most stylish holiday gold lame blouse, black satin pants, velvet holiday hat, and sent myself off to attend the Y-Me Holiday Lunch. I even put on lipstick and smile at everyone I talk to.

And I looked fabulous.

Wednesday, December 30th
By the way, lest you surmise, I've become entirely scrooge-like in my somewhat weakened and reclusive condition; I need to backtrack a bit and tell you what

a quintessential holiday we had in Northern Michigan last weekend, which is a Christmas miracle in and of itself.

Gaylord was enveloped in white snow.

We went out to dinner, all twelve of us, to "The Brown Trout" in Indian River. A place that is exactly like it sounds. We ate burgers and mashed redskins. My sisters enjoyed several rounds of pumpkin ale. We all sang along with the guitar player. The topic of cancer was left "outside" in the cold. At dinner, my sister Jenny toasted, "To Beth, may her strength and courage inspire us all." That was the most, and perhaps only, admirable thing my sister had ever said about me.

Mom and I shared some one-on-one time staying up late in the evenings sipping wine in the kitchen, talking about everything and nothing. It is stunning and odd, but "cancer" has been the best thing ever for our relationship, once distant and frigid. For the first time since I can remember, I felt like I had a mother.

Christmas with the family being kind to me: Priceless, Cancer: 0.

We went cross-country skiing, made holiday cookies, and sipped hot chocolate in front of the big fireplace, and for a few brief days, everything seemed right with the world. Most importantly, we celebrated my dear Grandmother Virginia's 89th birthday.

She squeezed my hand and said, "Elizabeth, you're my girl." Like a good quote, my grandmother can say so much by saying so little. She didn't need to tell me how much the letters meant to her, that they provided her with something to look forward to every week at the retirement "home" where she has begrudgingly lived for the past few years.

After my uncle sold her house in Birmingham, all her worldly possessions were claimed by her grandchildren, who moved in like a band of gypsies. Ginny went from riches to rags. Once again.

The retirement home was a run-down little place out in the sticks, as they say, run by a Korean doctor's wife, Natie, who didn't seem to like my grandmother too much. Natie wasn't accustomed to strong-willed residents. They engaged in a power struggle over everything, including the thermostat setting in my grand-mother's room, the time meals would be served and whether the windows would be cracked open or closed.

Ginny was relieved when one of the "grumpy old ladies," as she referred to the other residents, passed, and at last Ginny was able to have a room of her own with privacy to enjoy the company of her books. Even though her eyesight was failing, she managed to read voraciously and was usually in the middle of one that would be one of the following month's NYT's best sellers.

Her little corner of the world, as it had become, was a small and modest cedar paneled bedroom with worn carpeting and a daybed that she refused to lie down in. A maple chest of drawers housed the small wardrobe she required in the north woods. She spent most of her days and nights in an old recliner next to a small window that Natie eventually nailed shut. Above the daybed hung the tastefully framed commissioned portrait of Gretchen, the last remains of the grand life she once had. Gretchen, now in her late sixties, has been separated from Ginny for several years and lives in a home in Florida with other adults that require minimal care but looks down on her mother lovingly every day from her perch upon that paneled wall.

After our holiday and birthday celebration, I drove my grandmother back to the "Northwoods Residence," as she has dubbed it, where I helped her change into her nightgown and slippers. Not something I'd typically be comfortable offering. Proud of her self-reliance as she was, I knew she needed assistance when she asked for it. My facial expression must have said it all when I saw my eighty-nine-year-old grandmother nude.

"Oh, what are you staring at, Elizabeth...?" she still surprised me with her sharp wit. *"Someday your tits will be in your shoes, too."*

And that will be one of my fondest memories of my dear Grandmother Virginia.

It was a wonderful Christmas. For the first time I can recall in my adult life, I felt genuinely supported by my family. I lived with the distance and constant criticism for so long that I hardly realized how isolated I had been from all of them. It only took cancer to bring the family back together again.

As 1998 crawls to an end, I don't know whether to curse the year I was diagnosed with cancer... Or embrace it as the year that gave my life meaning.

Ten: No Mas

Friday, January 1st, 1999 8:26pm

*"The new year stands before me like a chapter
in a book waiting to be written."*

~ Unknown

I invited Maria over to the Blue House for dinner tonight. She arrived wearing her new wig and bearing gifts. A huge hand-painted Moroccan serving platter and three beautiful hand-made silk pillows, also from Casablanca.

I served broiled salmon, broccoli and green tea. After dinner, I told her there was a violin piece I wanted her to hear. I told Maria I had secretly been preparing myself for the Awful Possibility that could be ahead of me. Despite my "terrific" response to the therapy, the recurrence rates for IBC are so high. After the surgery and radiation, there may be a brief time for me to feel good and begin to look normal. My hair will grow back; my eyebrows and lashes will grow back. I may even feel attractive, living an everyday life again. And then it happens. Like it has with Shannon. Maybe it will show up as a backache, a headache or a dry cough. And the "choices" again. "Choices" no one deserves. More chemotherapy, disfiguring surgery, radiation and clinical studies. And eventually, hospice.

I have been secretly "designing" my funeral, I told Maria in strict confidence, but have not kept a written account of any of it. I'm almost ashamed that I have anticipated the end of my life with that amount of detail.

It would begin with a march through Grant Park to Lake Michigan, where my "inner circle" would board a sailboat with pink sails fluttering in the air and my ashes would be spread over the water. My sister Catherine would read a farewell letter I've composed to the people I loved. The celebration of my life would close with a quartet of violins playing "The Ashokan Farewell."

Maria and I sat on the sofa, closed our eyes and listened to the music but did not cry. "I don't think that is what Allah wants," Maria told me. "I think he wants you to come to visit me in Casablanca when I am well and back with my family." I told her I promised I would, but we know it isn't my promise to make.

10:04 pm
After Maria said goodbye, I put her in a cab. Then I listened to "The Ashokan Farewell" a few more times as I sweated profusely and fanned myself with a copy of "Menopause and the Mind."

I allowed myself to think about my "farewell" letter in which I beseech everyone to please get over the sentimental portion of the day and feel free to get rip-roaring tipsy and tell their favorite story of "remember when." I almost cringe thinking how my friends and family might fill in that blank at the would-be wake.

"Remember when Beth…" I can almost hear the sisters now.

Amy: "Tap danced to 'Singing in the Rain'"
Cathy: "…in the Miss Alpenfest Pageant."
Jenny: "At 22, though she hadn't taken tap lessons since she was six."
Cathy: "Didn't win said talent competition."
Amy: "Didn't even get Miss Congeniality."
Jenny: "Put Mom's wood-paneled Pinto into a lake on New Year's Eve."
Cathy: "Made Amy culottes out of our gingham bedroom curtains."
Jenny: "Broke mom's new Singer sewing machine in the process."
Amy: "Forced me to wear the un-hemmed curtain culottes to school."
Cathy: "Two words: Dippity-Do."
Jenny: "Plastered her hair with it and tweezed her eyebrows to death in 7th grade."
Cathy: "Looked like a bird in a helmet."
Jenny: "Was always late for…."
All: "EVERYTHING!"

Words of comfort I've heard at Gilda's recently are that people aren't gone until they are forgotten. I don't know that this is exactly how I would want to be immortalized, but I'm comforted to think I have at least given my friends and family things to smile about for some time.

"You never know how much space you occupy in people's lives."

~ F. Scott Fitzgerald

148

Saturday, January 2nd, 1999

All that reminiscing about how my sisters might immortalize me sent me sailing back in time again, trying to recall what caused me to enter the local beauty pageant in the first place.

It was anything but pretty.

My hometown, much like my dear Grandmother Virginia, is a paradox.

It promotes itself as a "cosmopolitan town." Yet, the only museum is the "Call of the Wild," where you follow painted bear tracks to view ancient stuffed animals in their "natural" habitats behind glass obscured by snotty-nosed children's fingerprints. The village aspires to uphold the tony image of our sister city, Pontresina, in the Swiss Alps. Yet, the two local ski resorts boast mostly "bunny hills" serviced by rope tows. And the "Swiss-inspired" cedar-shake shingled and stucco main street storefront are an ineffective disguise at best for the tavern, sporting goods store and the NRA card-carrying patrons who frequent them. The town is so progressive that the first "ethnic" restaurant opened was when I was eighteen, and the locals are still struggling with the pronunciation of empanadas and quesadillas to this day.

But every year, the annual "Alpenfest" brings out the town's very best, including the much beloved knobby knees competition, yodeling, pie eating and the like. And, as with any small-town festival worth its salt, the main attraction is most assuredly to determine what young maiden will be declared the fairest of them all. In Gaylord's case, the annual "Miss Alpenfest" pageant was the highly anticipated crown jewel of the annual festivities.

I never aspired to a sash and crown. Nor did the idea of traveling from a small-town to a small-town all summer long to wave at towns folk from an old convertible sandwiched between a Dairy Queen Float and the Knights of Columbus or Shriners on bicycles hold great appeal for me. At all.

Perhaps it was my utter lack of respect for the title blended with a hangover of adolescent disdain for the town that tortured my soul as a rebellious teenager. Resentment or apathy, whichever was to blame, the alpine pageant wagon was destined to go careening off the road, leaving me with nothing but a legacy of shame.

First, the bathing suit competition. Game over right from square one. Perhaps a heavy alpine fog deluded me into thinking just the right pair of support hose could make my thunderous thighs appear lithe and long instead of the lumpy German sausages they already were at the tender age of twenty-two.

Second. Talent competition. I should have withdrawn my "candidacy" based on this alone if the bathing suit sausage-fest wasn't sufficiently courting disaster. I had stacks of notebooks of short stories and a bulging portfolio of water-color and charcoal artistic renderings and even captured the coveted distinction of "Class Artist" (yes, out of a class of thirty-four). But faced with the quandary of how to entertain a gymnasium full of towns folks with a less subtle creative expression, I panicked. Out of sheer desperation, I turned to the single talent with entertainment value I had once cultivated: Tap Dancing.

I can almost hear my thought process again...Buy a used pair of shoes. Replace the tutu with a black bodysuit. Choreograph my rendition of a classic...Singing in the Rain. Yeah, that's the ticket!"

Again, I implore you, what was I thinking? Never mind that I was the laughing stock on the stage at the State Fair tap dancing at age six. Or that I knew nothing about choreography. That bona fide entertainment value I cleverly resuscitated was destined to become one of the greatest spectacles of self-humiliation in the Alpine village's one-hundred-year history and may even have made the front-page news over in Pontresina.

Last and hardly least was the panelist interview, a veritable piece of cake for any young lady with a thimble full of composure or quasi-sure-footed in a Q&A situation.

My voice still quivers to this day when I speak to an audience in a room with more than three people.

Here comes the wind-up question. Yes, it is a soft pitch. "What sights would you show me as a visitor to your community?" ... My mind raced, and my palms grew sticky as I thought how liberated I felt escaping the Alpine Village for college just a few years earlier, not to mention how culturally depraved I felt as an adolescent. The only thing I could think of was my mother's sage advice, for which she is widely revered throughout the cosmopolitan Alpine Village. "If you have nothing nice to say...don't say anything at all."

The panel of discerning and distinguished judges looked expectedly down their pointy noses and through their horned-rimmed coke bottle spectacles. A hush fell over the gymnasium.

Prolonged silence.

I forced an awkward smile befitting a beauty queen drop-out. And shrugged.

I might as well have been sitting in a dunk tank next to the runners-up from the knobby knees contest.

Facing breast cancer requires enormous courage, and I, of all people, will never make light of it. But tap dancing to your own rendition of "Singing in the Rain" at age twenty-two with sausage thighs and publicly displaying a lack of pride for one's hometown...

That's a unique strain of bravery that's hard to find.

Sunday, January 3rd, 1999
Well, at least the hot flashes have replaced nausea. I'll trade in my chronic vomiting for what's behind door number three, please, Alex.

While shopping for groceries today, I started sweating profusely again, like the Richard Nixon vs.- John F. Kennedy debate kind of profuse. But my sweat is no longer sweet and salty like it used to be after a hard run, which I haven't been able to do in four months. It was metallic. I was standing in Jewel, slumped over my shopping cart, sweating venomous poison. And as I stood there in my White Sox baseball cap and MSU sweatshirt hiding near the non-alcoholic beer, I started hot-flashing back to the Cynical Dr. Webber with her tail rattling, waiting to strike with the awful results of my most unfortunate mammogram. And then I remembered the bumper sticker I should have custom-ordered and thought the bumper stickers would have made clever stocking stuffers for the women in my Y-Me young survivors' group at the holiday lunch. And then my face suddenly feels hot and flush as if I've had the most spectacular toe-curling, hair-curling (if I had any) orgasm of my life, which certainly isn't the case since I'm as chaste as a Buddhist monk these days. And then I collapse into a child-like meltdown in front of the nonalcoholic beer, like a puddle of spoiled toxic chemicals, just as a cherubic stock boy rounds the corner in time to witness this. He politely asks if I'm feeling all right and do I need some water or fresh air.

And then I opened my mouth to speak against my better judgment.

The totality of the past five months comes spewing out with all the velocity of the fire hose last sprayed in my consultant with the Wise and Wonderful Dr. Cobleigh. But instead of fluid, the contents come out like barbed and jagged bits of a homemade bomb, as if I would even know what that was.

The sharp bits mixed with bullets and nails and shards of glass ricochet off the floor, beer bottles, and refrigeration case. Like a Main Street western shootout in front of the 'Ole Saloon. I see words (in no particular order or chronology) like "invasive," "aggressive," "radical," "mastectomy," "metastatic," "recurrence," and "depression." I even saw an errant and startling "suicidal" bouncing off the floor and ceiling. One particularly razor-sharp shard pierces me squarely in the heart: "Infertility."

The poor cherubic stock boy has fled the scene in search of someone of authority to "deal" with me before I frighten off innocent Sunday shoppers stocking up on Miller Light for the holiest-of-grail, football bowl and playoff games.

I pick myself off the floor, wipe my eyes and my dripping and bleeding nose with the sleeve of my MSU sweatshirt and hobble off, pushing my broccoli, green tea and non-alcoholic beer down aisle seven towards the checkout, consoling myself.

"...And sometimes, for short, we might have called her Cait."

Tuesday, January 5th, 1999
Sometimes change happens so gradually that it is barely perceptible.

I realize, as I keep comparing this journal to those of my past, how much I have changed in the past four months. I don't expect that every word and thought that flows through my fingertips is going to be thought-provoking or inspiring. I don't even expect that I will be able to seize every day I am lucky enough to be given. And I certainly don't take for granted the limited supply of days I may have to be grateful for in my future. I now understand that the three-year, five-year, and ten-year plans are, at best, aspirations. All this from the woman who reliably kept today's to-dos, this week's to-dos, and my year's top priorities color-coded.

I've come to accept that nothing is guaranteed except uncertainty.

The Franklin Planner – not to mention the Container Store and California Closets – is as full of false promises as any organized religion.

But the illusion of control... isn't it alluring?

Thursday, January 7th, 1999
Chicago's biggest winter storm since 1967.

The snow started falling on January first and didn't stop.

Nearly two feet of snow has smothered the city. Our neighbors have been cross-country skiing to the Blue Line to get to work. Our mailman resorted to snowshoes.

This morning I could hear the red-haired ADD kind from two doors down scream-ing with delight in a snowball fight with the other neighborhood kids emancipated by another Chicago Public School "snow day."

Despite the paralyzing effect the blizzard has had, there is something magical about piles and piles of snow that brings out the kid in most of us.

Including myself.

Fashionably clad in my pajamas, wool mittens and Timberland boots, I waded into the waist-deep snow in the backyard. I could almost taste the snowflakes on my bald head. I closed my eyes and let myself freefall into the virgin snow.

I remembered fainting into the pile of white towels just five months ago.

I felt like a different person, lying in my pajamas in the snow.

And I imagined myself as some large wanderlust bird, spreading my wings and flying high into the steely January sky and began moving my arms and legs and humming the lyrics of some Lenny Kravitz song, "I want to get away...I want to fly away...yeah...yeah...."

Careful not to mess with the snow imprint I just made, I stood up and admired my "Snow Angel." Later that afternoon, I photographed the winged girl and decided not to give her a name.

From the warmth of the Blue House, sipping my green tea, I have a perfect view of the young mulberry tree decorated with hungry wrens waiting for their turn at the bird feeder. Brave little birds surviving winter.

Speaking of birds, I read a poem written by a cancer survivor earlier this week called "Bird Poop,"

When a bird poops on you,
you won't forever become a person with bird poop.
It's just something that happened. Like cancer.
It happens. You get cleaned up. And move on.

~Unknown

In my case, I was standing in the place where Big Bird decided to take a massive sky dump.

Friday, January 8th

Project: Beth - Status Report:

Upon self-examination this morning, I think my right breast almost looks normal.

I realize how ironic it is that our relationship was defined by Breast Cancer, Dear Journal, yet I haven't referenced my actual breast often since my treatment began. I suppose I should feel weak and ashamed that I started taking showers in the dark and dressing in my closet after the diagnosis. As brave as I've tried to be, I was fearful of the visceral reaction I might have. For the past four months, I've been stuck in a gaper's delay on the Kennedy, but I haven't allowed myself to look at the accident for fear of what I might see.

This is lunacy because I AM the accident.

But today, after three months of chemotherapy and Herceptin treatments, I began gingerly running my hand along the side of what was once upon a time, my beautiful right breast. The whole breast was hard when I was diagnosed, like a saucer implanted in my chest. But this morning, I barely felt the edge of the imaginary plate. I know in my heart that the huge tumor has been gradually melting away like Dr. Cobleigh said ... like snow and ice from the longest winter in my life.

Saturday, January 9th

Hello, again, Dear Journal. Don't be blue. Blow dryers and hot rollers are dry and damaging. Name-brand conditioners and shampoos are overpriced, too. "L.A. Beth" in Journal Three had a lot of blond hair and she wasn't happy. No, not at all.

I remember... looking out of my office window at least three times a day, fixating on the furthest point I could see on the eastern horizon. It seemed, at the time, that there was nothing more tragic than feeling so far from home. I imagined seeing the Sears Tower and maybe even making out the John Hancock building if I squinted hard enough. Chicago. That's where I belonged.

I was looking out the window when my phone rang.

My worst fears were confirmed. Brian had fallen into a clinical depression that had become near life-threatening.

Not only did I kill our marriage... I was killing him.

I remember the great yoke of guilt. This was my responsibility. Or was it? What about my happiness? Where was that? How was it that my "new beginning" became the middle of such a train wreck?

Sunday, January 10th

I dreamed last night that the Dragon got locked in the old refrigerator in the basement. I found him curled up in the vegetable crisper next to a case of Coors Light. Lifeless and cold and moldy. I awoke with this guilt, and suddenly, in a state of half-consciousness but seemingly great clarity, I drew this parallel. This fire-breathing beast has oddly given me the new gift of a new perspective on life and so much liberation. And I will have to kill it, nonetheless.

I guess all is fair in Love, War, and Cancer.

Still, in a half state of consciousness, I see myself standing alone on the precipice under a jet-black sky. Suddenly the beast of all beasts appears and moves towards me, with jaws that bite and claws that scratch; the wind howls through my one again long. Fair-flowing hair and my French manicured nails glisten as I, looking all radiant and air-brushed, defiantly stare the Jabberwocky in his red eyes full of flames and heave the sword high in the air and hiss under my breath with vehemence...." Now off with your mother#$%@ing head!"

"Fairy tales are more than true, not because they tell us that Dragons exist, but because they tell us that Dragons can be beaten."
– Niel Gaiman

Monday, January 11th, 1999
Project: Beth – Status Report:
Denied chemotherapy due to low white blood cell counts
7th Herceptin infusion (my benevolent friend)
"Make-good" is January 18, aligning with the entire team consult

I didn't know whether to be relieved or disappointed.

Tuesday, January 12th, 1999
A truckload of bricks dropped on my head last night.

I made a nice dinner for Brian, as a surprise, for no reason. Something I haven't had the energy to do much as of late. He thanked me by saying I made him feel "important." And in that tiniest of moments, it suddenly felt so significant. But, of course! I've been so inside my own head. I have failed miserably in considering how this entire experience has been from Brian's point of view.

He feels forgotten or marginalized or second fiddle to "the Cancer."

As silly as it sounds, as part of my exercise in empathy this morning, I decided to put on his favorite White Sox baseball cap and his beat-up Converse high-tops and consider things standing in his shoes. I sat in the sneakers and Sox cap and waited for the eureka epiphany, expecting the feelings to flood over me.

Silence.

The ticking of the fifth anniversary Tiffany clock. A loud thud. A large bundle of insurance claim forms and medical bills sliding through the mail slot and landing on the foyer floor.

The truth is, the only thing I feel is silly sitting here in Brian's sneakers. But, I am still determined to understand this experience from his point of view.

Let's break it down, shall we? Imagine sleeping next to a bald woman who smells like poisonous sweat and is restless all night. Hardly recognizing this woman you once felt intimate with. Stripped of your manhood because you can do nothing to help her and you're even afraid to touch her. Imagine feeling the distance between you growing longer, like you're standing on the shore with cement blocks for feet and she's a canoe drifting out to sea.

Standing in his shoes is not easy.

Wednesday, January 13th, 1999
While I'm still feeling strong, before the next "Big" drug session, I need to come clean with you, Dear Journal. I've pink-washed the entire chemotherapy experience.

It is *not* the fairytale I told you about.

The City of Chemopolous is a dismal place no one wants to be, like a desolate roadside motel with plenty of vacancies. The Queen is a middle-aged, caring, and kind but somewhat disillusioned, would-rather-be medical author resigned to her thankless job in the chemotherapy ward. She is prone to colds and has a red nose; she has brown eyes and wears practical shoes and cardigans, like an earth mother. She treats me with kindness and dignity, but there is nothing retro-glamorous about the Land of the Living Dead. There are no tall ocean waves on the horizon or masts of a great pirate ship. There is no comfort in the familiarity of being assigned to the same recliner to receive the same bag of lethal poison used in the cold war

No. Not at all.

And as I listened to Henryk Gorecki's Symphony No. 3 of "Sorrowful Songs" this morning, I allowed the music to rise and wash over me and willed that it would annihilate the venomous pain I felt with the first wave of drugs coursing through my veins.

THE Pain.

The most profoundly unbearable Pain...like drowning in an infinite ocean of sorrow so deep it would take nearly two decades to describe...as the sordid water fills my lungs, I mourned everything I was about to lose, including the thing in this world I wanted the most. The tragic opera leads me to a dolorous place so filthy it snows black and is devoid of hope. The ground is littered with bones and human remains. The grief feasted on every cell in my body and soul, leaving my heart incinerated and my body emaciated. I thought of Joan of Arc being burned alive at the stake as the toxic chemicals burned like flames through my veins and ... Oh, The Glorious Pain.

The Glorious Pain felt like the highest note in the third movement as the bell tolls for all the millions of unjustly dead.

I threw in the wardrobe and stylized the entire experience to get through it.

"You never know how strong you are
until being strong
is your only choice."

~ Yogi Tea Bag

Thursday, January 14th, 1999

Dear Journal, I don't like to be tacky, and I've never been one to haggle, but I've been tracking each invoice and insurance claim form since that most unfortunate mammogram.

They have been pouring into our mail slot like a white-water river. I have a bill and claim forms for the entire cast of characters and all of the lovely "treatments."

And what a lineup it has been.

The Cynical Doctor, the Mousy Technician, Tan Dr. Tog, Decidedly North Shore Dr. Hartz 111, Stropping Doctor, Insensitive Idiot Intern, Painfully Honest Oncologist, Young Oncologist, Queen of Chemopolous and her Fresh Intern, the Wise and Wonderful Dr. Cobleigh, the scans, ultrasounds, x-rays, biopsies, FISH assay test, pathology, Adriamycin and Cytoxan infusions, anti-nausea medication, weekly Herceptin and daily Neupogen injections, the running tally on the cost of my care and treatments to-date is a whopping $171,101.40. It will be double that after my surgery and radiation. And probably triple when you throw in the plastic surgery, assuming I get that far.

Talk about adding insult to injury.

That could be a good topic for my next support group: "What could you have done with all of your Cancer money?"

For $200,000, I would buy a small lake. That same emerald lake I used to swim in as a kid. And I would make it a clothing optional beach. I'd invite all of my Chicago cancer friends to come and swim and sun without embarrassment or shame. And we would have alpine yodeling contests, feed the crusts from our baloney sandwiches to the fish and do cannonballs off the dock. And all would be right with the world.

Speaking of everything being right in one's world... Sunday night WGN did a story on Herceptin. They interviewed Carla, a woman I befriended in the waiting room at Rush a couple of weeks ago. She has experienced a complete remission of her metastatic breast cancer, which had spread to her liver, after a nine-year battle with the disease. There she was on the 9 pm news, absolutely beaming, two of her sons at her side, rosy cheeks, and a blue denim hat with pastel flowers reminding other breast cancer patients to "never give up hope."

Somehow, Carla's end became a new beginning in the middle of her life's biggest crisis.

On that note of inspiration and resilience, I've seen several variations of this printed on greeting cards and hanging in doctors' offices. Everyone feels entitled to change it, just a little, to include their favorite thing that cancer can't do.

What Cancer **Cannot** Do

Cancer is so limited.
It cannot shatter hope; It cannot cripple love.
It cannot kill friendship; it cannot suppress creativity,
It cannot take away memories.
It cannot silence courage…It cannot invade the soul.
It cannot conquer the spirit.

~ Author Unknown

After all, it is just a physical disease; we are so much more than our physical selves.

As long as I remember this, I have won my battle against cancer.

Sunday, January 17th

I'm nearing the end of the book, "Her-2." It has only taken me thirteen weeks to get through it. But it has hardly been an act of leisure reading. Whenever I come upon a fact, a stat, a date or anything I want to know more about, I do my online investigation. It is amazing how much medical information is floating out there, just waiting to be retrieved. I have an entire sub folder in "Project: BETH" dedicated to "Her-2" with sub-folders for the many investigators involved with the drug beyond Slamon…Ullrich, McGuire, Twaddle, Raab, Levinson, Curd, Shepard, Norton, Cobleigh, Visco, Erwin, Clark…and many more; trust me, I want to know who the real heroes are.

Herceptin cleared Phase I and two clinical trials in March '97, not quite two years ago. It was a "green light" for the final leg, Phase III, with the "pivotal" results expected by March last year. With those results, the data could be presented to the FDA, and the wheels could be put into motion for the drug's approval.

However, the timeline failed to consider a measure called "time to progression": the time between the beginning of treatment and the spread of metastatic cancer. When Genentech first planned the trial, it assumed that, on average, women treated for metastatic breast cancer would suffer a second recurrence nine months after they began treatment. Based on that assumption, the trial would have to fol-low the women for an entire year. However, since all the women in the test were

159

HER-2/neu positive, the highly aggressive nature of HER-2/neu-positive breast cancer meant that the trial could provide results five months earlier than planned. Genentech could apply to the FDA in the spring of 1998. Energized by this more agile timeline, Genentech devoted more staff to the HER-2/neu project.

Herceptin, the once "red-haired step-child," was elevated to Cinderella status.

At this point, I had to put the book down…the intricacy of the timing of my diagnosis and treatment was overwhelming. It is like the Universe was anticipating my plea bargain a decade before I was on my knees and then put a high-priority ticket on my request just months before I needed it.

Monday, January 18th, 1999

Project Beth: Status Report: Another Milestone
- Chemo make-good today.
- 8th infusion of Herceptin, second of Taxol
- Dr. Cobleigh felt "no palpable mass" in my breast today.

A mass that was ten centimeters at diagnosis, about the size of my entire breast, is gone to the human touch. To use the words, Dr. Cobleigh has used before, the tumor has just "melted away."

My entire medical team paraded into the room like a marching band, and words sprayed through the air like confetti. "Very gratifying," "Optimistic," "Miraculous," and "Best response we could have hoped for." "Herceptin is truly a godsend," Dr. Cobleigh adds as an exclamation to all the chatter. The Sensitive Surgeon almost used the c-word. "Our goal is for a complete response. Any stray cells have been pulverized for such a large mass to be eradicated."

I like "pulverized."

Herceptin and chemotherapy evidently may be the new one-two punch!

In my giddiness, I contemplate doing a victory dance to the "Eye of the Tiger." On the ceiling. Nude! But then I exhale slowly and drift back to earth like a day-old helium balloon.

The cold reality is that cancer cells may still be present, although they can't be felt. And even in a best-case scenario, none of this eradicates the possibility of an eventual recurrence. There are no statistics and no studies to help ground our expectations. "Sailing in uncharted waters," Dr. Cobleigh herself has said.

Still, those three words are like a symphony to me.

"The earth has music for those who listen."

~ William Shakespeare

Eleven: Celibacy Aside, Will We Die...?

Tuesday, January 26th

My sister Catherine responded to an e-mail I sent her yesterday. She said she enjoys reading my letters; I have "an easy way with words." One of the nicest compliments I've ever received from her.

Catherine and I think a lot alike, talk alike and write alike. Catherine and I are, in fact, a lot alike. Both introspective, perfectionists, critical, outwardly self-sufficient, inwardly deeply sensitive and sentimental, and sometimes thorny, especially in the morning. Did I mention determined? Catherine has the determination that could outrun-run a rabid dog. In fact, she was attacked by one on a back-road training run at mile five and then continued to run another seven with her back lacerated and bleeding because she thought it was "a test from the Universe" to see if she was "made of the mettle it takes to run a marathon."

I kid you not.

Despite my gratifying response, I thought that if I were one of the many IBC warriors that died in combat, I would want the worn, torn, and water-stained Journals to have a good home.

I want to entrust my journals to Catherine.

I would ask that she give special treatment to my first water-speckled and much-misunderstood journals and that its frayed, embroidered jacket and blue suede spine would have a special place on a high shelf, kept company by the middle children, the warped and tear-stained sea foam green and permanently fractured mocking moon. The youngest and most sensitive "Full Circle" would bookend the group. And this journal, yet to be named, taken to completion as a tribute to the author, a hardcover published book that now and then escapes from the shelf to the coffee table as the focus of the melancholy but fond conversation.

I wonder how different the direction of my life might have been had I just circumvented all that soul-searching and introspection that live in my journals. Why couldn't I have been a simple girl and written about superficial mindless shit?

If only life came with a rewind button.

I'd tell young Beth… "Put the pen down and back away from the journals…slowly."

Wednesday, January 27th

Today, a note from a twenty-year survivor reminded me of the positive aspects of having cancer.

> I was given a gift, wrapped shabbily.
> In it, I found courage I never knew existed.
> And patience far beyond anything I've ever experienced.
> I was given the ability to trust a stranger with that dearest to me
> And endurance for the unknown.
> I was given the unconditional love of family and friends,
> I was given a fond farewell of my modesty and vanity,
> Acceptance and devotion of an imperfect body.
> I was given a solid shoulder to lean on.
> Laughter and good times, more special than ever before.
> I was given many new friends,
> Incredible, courageous women I am proud to know.
> I was given warm sunshine, beautiful green grass, bland blue skies
> And sparkling city lights.
> I was given things to see that once before were ignored.
> I was given every glorious day to enjoy, every month to savor,
> Every year to rejoice.
> I was given the gift of Life. I was given breast cancer.

I know I've been vacillating between "it's a gift" and "it's a horrible life-threatening disease" as of late, and the sentiment is special, but if breast cancer is a gift, I'm returning it. I don't care whom it offends. Please check reason(s) for return:

1. induces emotional trauma
2. disfiguring
3. other: resulting in infertility, celibacy, insomnia and other unpleasant side effects

January 28th

Dear Journal, so what's new? Do you believe that now it's my turn to be rescued? Drifting back again, perusing "Journey of a Soul." The moon still mocks me from the cover. Towards the latter half of the journal is a subtitle: "The Rescue Mission."

Brian had been under the care of an excellent doctor helping him gradually pull back the darkness that had engulfed him and threatened his job and every aspect of his life.

I would board a plane on Friday afternoon back to Chicago and return on the 6 am flight on Monday mornings. Landing at LAX by 8 am PCT time. I could make it to McCann on mid-Wilshire by 930a, f I avoided the 405 and took my surface street shortcut.

I did that as many weekends as I possibly could. Brian was finally getting better. I remember one of the last legs of the rescue mission.

After meeting at the airport, Brian and I drove downtown so that he could keep his haircut appointment at the place on Pearson Street. We met up afterward at the bookstore on Michigan Avenue, where we browsed the aisles and found ourselves in the children's section reading some of our favorites together, laughing so loudly we were scolded by a sales clerk and bounced out of Borders Books!

We tended the garden and yard at home and put out the patio furniture. We grilled chicken. Brian set the table with our wedding china and a bouquet of Iris he had waiting for me. We dined by candlelight on the patio, stared at the stars and talked about the future.

We decided that after everything we had been through, we'd be better off together again.

In Chicago. It seemed fitting.

And that became the beginning of our "middle."

Monday, February 1st, 1999
Project: Beth – Status Report:
- No chemo again today. My WBS's still pretty paltry.
- 9th Herceptin infusion.

Kind of like Soup Nazi, only toxic chemicals were denied instead of a steaming cup of cream of asparagus. After making a human pin cushion out of me, I did get my weekly "fix" of Herceptin, thankfully. The nurse joked that I was having a "bad vein day." My mother-in-law, who has made a point of attending every chemotherapy session with me, added, in her well-intending way, that I couldn't have a "bad hair day," so I had a lousy vein day instead.

Ah, levity.

For the past two weeks, I have been planning our "Vacation from Cancer." Surfing the internet, scouring the travel section of the Tribune, and asking friends for the ultimate destination recommendation. My screen saver has become a cliff-side view of the Pacific, as seen from Playa del Ropa, Zihuantanejo. La Casa Que Canta, the house that sings.

Enough said. We planned a perfect excursion to sunny Mexico for mid-March, right after my final treatment of chemotherapy. We will board a plane and leave any residual traces of cancer in Chicago for five days.

Five glorious days.

(Oooff!)

Not so fast. Right hook to the stomach.

"I'd seriously rethink any plans to go to Mexico," the Well-Intending Nurse advised me. "Your immune system is too weak."

I imagine special effects: The angelic choir emanating from the house on the cliff abruptly halts like someone scratching a record. Heavy, dark clouds cover the entire sky. Mexico is cast in complete darkness as a total eclipse of the sun is performed on cue.

"Do you have children?" The Well-Intending Nurse changes gear abruptly.

More special effects: I am now covered with open wounds, and she is holding a giant saltshaker and a wedge of lime over my head. I struggle to suppress the knee-jerk response BOOMING over the intercom inside my head:

I WAS BEGINNING TO TRY AND GET PREGNANT WHEN I GOT CANCER...! I AM HAVING HOT FLASHES, IN ADDITION TO ALL THE OTHER LOVELY SIDE-EFFECTS OF CHEMOTHERAPY...! AM IN MENOPAUSE AT THE AGE OF THIRTY-SEVEN...CHILDREN WERE THE ONE THING IN LIFE I WANTED MOST...! CAN NOT EVEN BEGIN TO MOURN THE LOSS OF NOT BEING ABLE TO HAVE CHILDREN BECAUSE MY SURVIVAL IS THE ONLY THING I CAN FOCUS ON...

Instead, I politely offer the minimal requirement, "No, we don't have any children."

"Then you don't have to worry about canceling a babysitter," the Well-Intending Nurse consoles.

Ah, yes. This fragmented fantasy is not such a big deal. However, if a babysitter were involved, that would be a real tragedy!

The bag of Herceptin drips its last drop. I say a cheerful goodbye. "See you next week." I walked out of the room and passed the Well-Intending Nurse with my thought bubble blinking in neon yellow:

"I am SO going to Mexico."

Friday, February 5th
Today was one of those "just put one foot on the floor" mornings. But now that I've joined the land of the living, it almost feels warm enough to sit on the back porch. Fifty-three degrees, they report. I am sitting in the ugly purple pajamas looking at my neglected flower beds, thinking that before I know it, the crocus will push their way up, followed by the daffodils and the red tulips.

The hundred beautiful red tulips. When I planted them last fall, I wondered if I'd see them bloom.

There was an interesting dialogue on my favorite TV show Monday night. A young boy was dying of cancer. He asked a lawyer if he could sue.

"Whom do you want to sue?" the attorney asked.

"God." He replied. "I want to sue God."

Then, upon seeing the blank expression on the attorney's face, the dying, bald little boy has a sad realization. "OH, no. There is no God. Just like Santa Claus."

We believe because we need to. We believe life has a deeper meaning because the thought that life might be pointless is just too....

Wednesday, February 10th
Last night, Brian was working on a photo album, lovingly preserving our memories, picture by picture. "This is you, right before your second treatment," he said proudly and sweetly, and then, as somebody laid the last straw on his back, his body slumped over in the chair. "...You have to make it through this so we can look back at these pictures together...." His shoulder began to shake, and I knelt and put my arms around him.

"I will. I promise." I ached and wished to God I had the right to say it. "…but it's not my promise to make."

"Don't cry because it's over.
Smile because it happened."

~ *Dr. Seuss*

I can only hope that is how Brian might eventually feel if I run out of options in my fight. If only I had given him more photo albums full of happy memories and been a better wife. He deserves so much better than the pain I've caused.

Both in sickness and in health.

Friday, February 12th, 1999
Today is Flower Friday. Brian has brought me flowers every Friday since I started treatment. Every bouquet is uniquely different. Today it was "Birds of Paradise" in anticipation of the Mexico Cancer getaway we had planned.

He hasn't been able to make many of the chemotherapy sessions. Nancy "stands in" his place. The Advertising pressures have been more intense, and I think he worries that if I lose my job or have to take something less stressful and lower-paying, it will be his job to be the sole breadwinner.

I haven't given him enough affirmation for everything he has done. He steadies the needle and helps me give myself the daily Neupogen shots my body now requires to keep my white bold cell count high enough to continue with my therapy. He gives me a cheerful "thumbs up" every morning when he leaves for work and tells me I am perfect, perfect for him, and soon Cobleigh will pronounce me perfect, too. When I tell him I might have to leave again, but against my will, he says he knows the Universe will let me stay. When I ask him how he can be so sure, he sends me a card that says: "I'm closing my eyes and holding out my arms."

The same thing he said when I was deciding to come back to Chicago, back to him. Through it all, Brian has stayed upbeat. But then, I wouldn't expect anything less from him.

Brian Patrick Grady: 408, Cancer: 0.

Saturday, February 13th
I looked in the mirror today and didn't recognize myself.

I have been in purple pajamas for three days. As much as I hate to admit it, this chemotherapy thing has kicked the living shit out of me. It happened so gradually with the hair loss, the missing eyebrows, and eyelashes, the weight loss - which under different circumstances I might have appreciated - the graying complexion.

Today, it hit me like a truckload of bricks. I look like a certified cancer patient.

This won't do!

I summoned all the strength I had left. I peeled off my ugly purple pajamas, showered, and dressed in one of my Ann Taylor suits, which was almost falling off me. I donned my fabulous navy-blue hat and called for a taxi cab to go window-shopping on the Gold Coast, where I got the courage to go into a very upscale boutique. To look. Not much is in my disability budget these days.

As I roamed the upscale boutique brimming with "just the thing" for "someone who has everything," a little pewter box caught my eye. It looks like a miniature war chest, battered and tarnished, in an honorable way. I imagine it must be nearly a hundred years old. Something in what I recognize as Latin or Italian, I am not sure which, is etched on the lid, "Tutto E Possible." Intrigued, I pick up the pewter box to examine it more closely. As I lift the top, I see it inscribed on the inside…

"Anything is possible."

So, today it was a little pewter box that made me cry – which I promptly purchased with the last $117.03 in my checking account, satisfied it was a wise investment for a reminder that anything IS possible.

Sunday, February 14th
Roses are red; violets are blue; cancer is character-building, and so are you. I ate oatmeal, drank tea today, and wrote a silly poem to celebrate this romantic holiday.

Green Tea
You can't ever be alone when you love yourself
And you know you do...
When you wouldn't trade places with another cancer-free person
For all the green tea in China

You know, Dear Journal, I'm doing my best not to be cynical on this of all holidays. But it's not lost on me that the Universe has a penchant for irony. Advanced-stage cancer for a woman who has made a point of planning every aspect of her life. No opportunity for early detection for a woman who took excellent care of her health and was proactively getting annual mammography screenings since the age of thirty. Chemotherapy for a woman who clung to her long, thick beautiful hair like a security blanket since her early teens. A mastectomy for a woman who always felt she had the perfect B-cup but never flaunted her breasts. A biological clock hurled at the wall when we were seeking prenatal consultation and planning, at long last, to start a family.

But, somehow, I believe it will be okay because I have the most precious things. I've discovered a profound awareness of and appreciation for the little things. I've learned not to sweat the small stuff - and it IS primarily small stuff. But most importantly, I've learned to believe that no matter what: Love Prevails. I've seen it repeatedly - in the waiting room, in my support groups and in every day.

It was there all along. I just couldn't see it before.

Wednesday, February 17th
I wanted to stay in bed all day. But I forced myself to put one foot on the floor, and before I knew it, I was sitting in my Gilda's Club support group.

The group is a hodge-podge of cancers covering all parts of the body. You name it; someone in the group has it. What almost fascinates me is how insidious and ironic the diagnoses are. It is like God was sitting around having a couple of beers with a few buds and started coming up with hilarious diagnoses just for fun.

"...YOU, THE YOUNG SINGER IN THE ROCH BAND WHO DOESN'T SMORE DOPE, I'M GIVING YOU THROAT CANCER. (HA, HA, HA). AND YOU, THE LESBIAN WHO FINALLY CAME OUT OF THE CLOSET AND FOUND A LIFE PARTNER WITH WHOM YOU EXPLORED ARTIFICIAL INSEMINATION, FOR YOU, OF COURSE, OVARIAN CANCER. (HA, HA, HA) AND, LET ME SEE, YOU, YOUNG LADY, WHO NEVER SMOKED A CIGARETTE IN YOUR LIFE, YOU SHALL DEVELOP DOUBLE LUNG CANCER (HA, HA, HA)..."

Today's moderated topic was sexuality and cancer, which seemed to interest the usually quiet members more.

Especially the guys.

Fred, the Rock star with throat cancer, isn't getting any but is jerking off plenty; he can't swallow because of all the radiation to his tracheae, he laughs, but his hands work just fine.

Gail, the lesbian with Ovarian, isn't able to think of sex at a time like this and fears her partner might start cheating on her.

Jane, a stage one breast cancer patient – who wears her bandanas and a t-shirt that says, "Fuck Cancer" like a status symbol – hasn't let it slow her down. She's grateful she doesn't have to worry about waxing down there and finds it helps to us lubricant and get high.

Predictably, as it always does, the topic boomerangs back to the inevitable and the one thing we truly all have in common: Celibacy aside, Will we die?

Gail with Ovarian asks, "At what point do you begin to feel like you've beaten cancer? After five years? Ten years?

"When I die from something else," I offer. The group laughed. It felt good.

Friday, February 19th
I had lunch with Shannon today. She invited me to her apartment at One East Delaware. We had so much to catch up on since the holidays.

She answered the door looking stunning, as she always does, simply wearing faded jeans and a white blouse. We warmed up over tea and scrapbooks, and eventually, Shannon got the courage to show me what she wanted to talk about. She retrieved a large envelope from her desk, and I knew what I was about to see before she said a word: Images from her recent CT scans showing more spots on her liver and a few new ones in her bones.

"I tested negative for HER2 over-expression, Beth." Shannon begins with the bottom line. "Herceptin isn't an option for me. I have decided not to have any more chemotherapy. I'm seeing an herbalist and will pursue alternative therapy. The most important thing to me is to enjoy the time I have. I don't want to spend it bald in a hospital with needles stuck in me like a pin cushion. I plan on travel-ing and sailing and seeing more of the world, and when I run out of money and strength, I will spend my time doing outreach and public speaking, and at the very end, when all I can do is sit, I will write and paint...I've always wanted to learn how to paint...."

There was nothing I could say. There it was. What she had left of her life was all pragmatically charted out.

After I left Shannon's apartment, I took the long way home through the park. It is an unreasonably mild day for mid-February, I notice. As I drove along Cannon Drive, the rain started to fall. All I could think about was that x-ray. One picture with a few little spots changed everything.

173

A somber procession of black silhouettes moved across the forbidding grey sky. The barren trees seemed to be drooping with the oppressive weight of February. Everything about the day looks and feels and smells austere.

I opened my sunroof and drove the rest of the way home with the numbing winter rain pouring in. And, suddenly, laughing at cancer felt like the most inappropriate response I could have ever imagined. And I cried for Shannon and myself and all of the senseless injustice in the world. I called so long I thought I might cry my eyes right out of my head.

I would do anything to change the vile plan the Universe allowed to be set in motion.

Twelve: How The Journals Got Their Spots

Monday, February 22nd

PROJECT: BETH - Status Report

- 3rd round of Taxol.
- WBC is down on the edge of another delay, we decided to push it.
- 11th Herceptin infusion
- Met with the medical team to discuss surgery.
- Final chemotherapy will be on 3/17. Yes, on St. Patrick's Day.

I feel like I've been crawling across the desert toward this "finish line." Although intellectually, I know there is a possibility this isn't the finish line for me. According to those annoying statistics or lack thereof, depending on how you look at it, as an Inflammatory Breast Cancer patient sailing in uncharted waters.

For the quote book:

*"If my ship should sail from sight, it doesn't mean my journey ends.
It simply means the river bends."*

~ Enoch Powell

And, randomly, the ship analogy reminds me that my father once told me the Eskimos euthanized the sick and elderly by putting them in a canoe and pushing them out to sea with a jug of water and a loaf of bread. If that was an option for me, I'd ask that my last meal be a full-bodied California Cabernet and a wheel of brie as they shove my canoe out to sea.

Tuesday, February 23rd, 1999

I wasn't ready to talk about it yet. Yesterday's consult around the surgery that is. Today I am feeling more sure-footed. The surgery will be scheduled right after Easter: a modified radical mastectomy.

No reconstruction.

I've been fighting with my insurance company, as they will not pay for immediate reconstruction. It isn't "customary" for IBC patients. Most patients have a local recurrence that interrupts reconstruction due to more radiation anyway.

I bravely announced that it's just "skin and tissue I can live without." In twenty-eight days, I will have one breast. There will be a big red scar where my right breast now proudly hangs.

Wow.

I've heard it said that scars are like tattoos with a more interesting story.

> *"A powerful woman accepts the war she went through*
> *And is ennobled by her scars."*
>
> *Carly Simon*

That "it's skin and tissue I can live without" proclamation sounds brave in your oncology team's presence. And I suppose a "cosmetic" issue seems a little trivial when you are fighting for your life. But it's like saying goodbye to an old friend. After almost seven months of anticipation, did I believe the mastectomy would be...*liberating?*

I've always fancied my breasts as one of my better assets. A nice B-cup, not too big that they jiggle around too much or gets in my way, but enough that they fill out a bathing suit with a tasteful amount of cleavage. I remember my first training bra at eleven, well before my best friend, and how jealous she was. I remember the boys in my class noticing my development, and I coyly pretended not to notice them noticing. Then there was the fashion show I would perform for myself when no one was home, and I'd sneak into my parent's bedroom, sort through my mother's lingerie drawer, and sashay around in her lacy black push-up bra. And I remember the first time the girls got "felt up" by my seventh-grade boyfriend in the dark anonymity of the local movie theater. Ah, and how very flattered I felt at the Indianapolis 500 one year when I bravely went bra-less, and some 300-pound shirtless and sunburned Hoosier yelled, "nice hooters." Or, tits. He probably said "tits."

The point is, my breasts were always my friends, and I am getting sentimental and sad knowing I'm sending one off to war, never to be seen again.

Speaking of old friends missing in action, a high school friend, Monica, called today to let me know she is also going through breast cancer. Her surgery was just last week. She doesn't have medical insurance and cannot afford reconstruction. To make her situation even more daunting, she is divorced and going through this alone.

I was in awe of her strength as she said with conviction…."And after I get this all behind me, Beth, I will find an extraordinary man…with one hand."

Wednesday, February 24th
Despite all the positive news and progress, I've been thinking about mortality again. It's so difficult to "trust" any medical information I receive. I honestly do want to trust my doctors. But it's so difficult. After being told my mammogram was normal, just seven months before being diagnosed with a ten-centimeter tumor. Not to mention a normal routine breast exam two months before my breast became red and swollen.

And so, I've been thinking about - obsessing about - death.

When you think about it, the "worst case scenario" – departing this life in my thirties – might not be so bad. I've never really fancied the idea of getting old.

There's nothing dignified about it.

Tucked away, like my dear grandmother, in some poorly furnished rest home with a bunch of forgotten old farts. Soft, bland food. Long days and even longer nights. Worrying about what diseases you might get and watching friends get those diseases you are so frightened of. Feeling like the world is spinning faster and you can no longer keep up. And then you start to give up. A little more each day. And worse of all, how lonely each day is. Gradually, you stop hoping for letters, telephone calls and visitors. You accept the fact that you have become conveniently "forgotten."

And all you can do for mental stimulation and decent company is read novels. Until your eyesight fails you.

Right now, at age thirty-seven with a supportive husband and my wits and, for the time being, both of my breasts, perhaps this is as good as it gets.

Except for that (annoying) cancer part.

Thursday, February 25th
Hate to be a downer, but I'm stuck on death again today.

Brian isn't exactly a deep thinker, most of the time, but he must be contemplating the possibility of life alone, again. A time when he goes to bed, and there is no sick woman next to him. Waking up in the morning, rolling over to an empty space, and making two cups of coffee instead of four on Sunday morning. Would he contact Ann Taylor and tell them to stop sending catalogs, or would he let them keep coming? Would he donate all my clothes to Good Will, for that matter? I wonder how long it would take him to change the outgoing message on the answering machine. What about my coffee mug collection? Would it just be too painful to see reminders of me in every cupboard and every drawer? Would he begin to let go of those pieces that remain of me a little bit more until I eventually live on only in the photo albums? And, how long would it take for our friends to start mentioning this remarkable woman they know and subtly suggest a double date?

I can't help but wonder... how long would it take for me to become donated, erased, and replaced?

Friday, February 26th
Ironically, or conveniently – or both – tonight, the main topic in my support group at Gilda's Club was mortality and the possibility that we might die from our disease. No beating around the bush like last week.

"We might not live this way," our group leader gestured as she stretched her arms out in front of herself, indicating length. "But we *all* have the opportunity to live like *this*," ....and she stretched her arms out again, indicating width.

The words fell right out of my mouth.

"Live W I D E," I said. "We can all *Live W I D E.*"

We all looked at one another, stunned by the profundity of the concept. The room was respectfully quiet for several minutes. Then in a powerful moment I will never forget, we all stretched our arms out together and repeated in unison, "Live W I D E."

"The greatest obstacle to living is expectancy,
which hangs upon tomorrow and loses today...

The whole future lies in uncertainty: Live immediately."

~ Seneca

Saturday, February 27th
As the tedium of February and her rain abate, I decide that if there were three days in this calendar month, the lousy month would have been precisely three

days too long. Except for the thirty-three minutes I spent with Patricia with her daughter Grace earlier this week in the waiting room at Rush.

Grace is dying of lung cancer at the age of twenty-two.

Grace has spent the past three years confined to a wheelchair and in and out of hospitals as if it were routine for a young girl her age. Young Grace strikes me as a cross between a beautiful but frail caged flamingo and the Old Mulberry Tree, with her sturdy roots standing steadfast and magnificently, mortality fluttering in the distance. Patricia, her mother, looked like she hadn't slept one night in those three years. She has taken her daughter to every specialist in the country at all of the top cancer centers ... John Hopkins, Sloan Kettering, MD Anderson, and Mayo Clinic. Finally, Patricia found a doctor here at Rush who may be willing to do a double lung transplant on Grace. She and Grace came here hoping for that (last) chance.

I sat listening to every word Patricia shared about their heartbreaking journey while Grace sat breathing in and out in whispers, somehow looking serene with the apparatus strapped to her porcelain face.

My diagnosis and treatment seemed trite compared to what Grace and Pat have faced.

"Never give up. No matter what statistics they throw at you, always put yourself in the top percent. No one deserves it more than you and Grace. " My words seem to fall flat on the waiting room floor, thin and inadequate like a used tissue. But Grace smiled at me, anyway. Impossibly poised and peaceful in her cage of plastic tubing, unjustly tethered to the ground by her oxygen tank and wheelchair.

An incarcerated flamingo.

When Pat looked away for a moment, Grace reached over and touched my hand and said in an intense whisper, "Thank you for making my mom feel better."

Grace was aptly named.

Add this to the tally of victories I've seen from my seat in the oncology waiting room.

Pat & Grace: 227, Cancer: 0.

"Be a flamingo in a flock of pigeons.
The world needs more grace."

– EMC

Monday, March 1st

Carol from California called last night. One of her friends, also in her thirties, has just been diagnosed with breast cancer, and she was hoping I might have a few words of hope and encouragement to pass along. "What is the best advice you've been given?" was her question.

Without a second of hesitation, the words shot out of my mouth.

"Listen to the Music."

Carol seemed a little confused. Was there a specific genre of music I listened to that was incredibly calming? No, I explained. It was like the act of crying. It was about being aware of and deeply moved by the beauty surrounding us every day by paying attention to the most minor and seemingly insignificant details.

I explained that it is a metaphor for my new brand of Carpe Diem: Living Wide.

Carol seemed a little perplexed but appreciative.

Today I am sitting at my pine desk, studying the simple greeting card on brown recycled paper with the lone ballerina. This simple card has become my touchstone. The dancer has a fire in her eyes, yet her pose reflects exquisite discipline and grace. The inside of the card was originally blank.

I don't know the sender, the 20-year survivor, a friend of a friend. Pam. We've never met, spoken, or had any communication save the singular card that sits like the North Star on my desk.

I imagine Pam leafing through a manila file folder of greeting cards she keeps in stock, an arsenal at the ready, thoughtfully collected one by one. I imagine Pam taking a deliberate detour with her shopping cart down the greeting card aisle on her weekly grocery trips. I imagine Pam sitting at her desk in a modest but warm apartment that beckons in a soft accomplished voice...a strong, independent woman lives here. I imagine Pam pausing, looking up at a ticking Eiffel Tower wall clock, smiling as the perfect sentiment dawns on her and she inscribes the blank card with conviction...

"Beth, *LISTEN to the music.*"

If Pam only knew how her words have inspired me.

Tuesday, March 2nd
Dearest Journal, I forgot to mention some exciting news earlier.

The Director of Gilda's Club asked me to take part in a review of Non-for-Profits being considered as the beneficiary of Northwestern University's annual Dance Marathon. It is one of the largest and most well-established student-run philanthropies in the country.

The "pitch" was today.

They were hearing well-rehearsed presentations from major powerhouse organizations, including Make-A-Wish Foundation and United Way, to select the beneficiary for 2000. Quite a lot was at stake. Gilda's Chicago chapter has been struggling financially since it opened a year ago. They could reap half a million if selected, covering the club's operating costs for several years. The review was so vital that they were flying in Joanna Bull, Radner's cancer psychotherapist, co-founder and executive director of Gilda's Club from New York.

Gilda's Club stacked up against some of the largest NFPs in the country with compelling cases and polished presentations. I felt relieved that my role was more of a "prop." I just had to sit there and look like a cancer patient, something I'm pretty qualified to do these days.

As I traversed the campus, watching the well-bundled students beelining to their lecture halls, I remembered how full of plans and aspirations I was just fourteen years ago as a graduate student on a different campus, so unaware of the left turns ahead.

When I reached the student assembly hall where I was meeting Brian, the director of the Chicago chapter, Laura Jane, looked flustered. At first, I was sure it was because I was running late.

"Joanna's flight got delayed. She isn't going to make it. She was going to lead the presentation, so we needed to improvise. We don't want to put you on the spot, Beth, but do you think you could present a member's perspective of Gilda's Club?"

For a second, I felt a pit in my stomach. I thought a frail bald girl in a silly hat would come off like a homespun barn dance compared to what the powerhouses would unveil. But the pit was replaced by a surge of determination. I grabbed Brian's arm and headed into the auditorium.

This was my chance to harness the mother f&%$#ing cancer (pardon my French) and use it for something good.

And that's precisely what I did.

I can't tell you what I said verbatim. Well, I could, but that's not the point here. It was a hybrid of a sales pitch I might have done a year ago as an Advertising professional and an emotional enema, which I am more prone to these days.

I tried to connect with the students by talking about how being on campus made me recall my college days and all my plans, including a successful career, meeting a great guy and having a family. I talked about how cancer changed some of that, except for the great guy part, as I squeezed Brian's hand.

I spoke about how the "red door" is a gateway to a place that feels like a close friend's home, where you can feel "comfortable" having cancer. After all, at Gilda's Club, cancer is the norm. No one treats you like you have an affliction, and you don't have to worry about using the "c-word" tentatively. It is a place where laughing at cancer is okay. It might not be suitable for everyone, but at the right moment, it can be powerful. I emphasized that cancer doesn't just happen to a person; it happens to your whole family and everyone who loves you. I talked about how important the club had become for Brian and the family support group that he attended. I spoke about all of the classes and resources the Club offers its members and how all of this is available to the Club's members for free. I joked that you only need to have Cancer to belong! I told the students that Gilda's Club is an assembly of courageous people we are proud to call friends. Emphatically, I told the committee that by choosing Gilda's Club, they would make a big difference for the small but growing club and help keep the red door on Wells Street open for years to come.

My cell phone rang about ten minutes after Brian and I left the assembly hall.

Northwestern unanimously selected Gilda's Club as the beneficiary.

As our car glided along the snowy Lake Shore Drive, I felt a warm glow that radiated from my head to my toes. And I smiled *all the way home.*

> *"Cancer gave me membership in an elite*
> *club…I'd rather not belong to."*
>
> ~ Gilda Radner

186

Thursday, March 4th

I'm still smiling two days later.

Harnessing the Cancer is more potent than laughing at it. The whole experience strikes me as a perfect example of my new philosophy: Living Wide. Perhaps something philanthropic could be in my future! It would certainly help more folks than my introspective journaling.

I'm ready to start living fully in the present again. I've tried my best to make sense of the messiness in the past. But you know what?

LIFE IS MESSY.

It just is.

I leaf through the last blurry and water-stained pages of "Journey of a Soul," determined to lay the old journals to rest. But the pages beckon, pulling me away again from the present…

For most of us, a few things happen just once in a lifetime.

One extraordinary love (okay, perhaps more if you are extremely fortunate or patient), one moment of fame, and one crown jewel during one's career.

McCann was mine.

My career highpoint, not my soulmate.

Blue chip boss I liked and respected. Prestigious client roster that included Sony Entertainment, Nestle, Cathay Pacific, among others. A collaborative creative team and account planners who understood media, and account executives who stayed respectfully out of the way. I was on the shortlist of every media sales rep in town, which meant well fed and entertained. But, most importantly, we had a fantastic team of forward-thinking media talent, and the camaraderie we shared was genuine. I invested so much of myself into my job at McCann. It was the sole thing that kept me sane in the Vortex. They promoted me, nominated me for an international leadership academy and planned to send me to Copenhagen.

While those things were professionally validating at the time, they weren't nearly enough to keep me there. I needed to go "home" and rebuild my life with Brian.

As I sat in the General Manager's spacious office, expecting to deliver a polished resignation speech, what fell out of my mouth was simply: "I thought I came here wanting more, but I learned, sometimes less is more. I quit."

The General Manager said, "Shit."

And that was it.

My farewell note to my colleagues said something to the effect of:

"For those who may have thought I was a little different, this provides confirmation. I am trading in my view of the Hollywood sign for one of the Chicago River in February."

Had I known what lay in store for me after returning "home" to Chicago, I could have appended the farewell memo.

"I will also be getting cancer, re-marrying my now not-so-depressed ex husband, and living happily-ever-after, just like they say in Hollywood!"

Friday, March 5th

Today in my Y-Me "Under 40" group, we talked about intimacy and breast cancer, fears about body image, femininity and sexuality.

With my impending surgery and the loss of my right breast still conveniently categorized as a "cosmetic issue" in the right hemisphere of my head ... this is stuff I need to hear.

There was quite a bit of pent-up demand for this topic. The dialogue started immediately bubbling over the top without stirring the pot.

Sally, forty-one, is the longest-term member or "elder" in the group; we keep her age under wraps because we all like her immensely and the well of information she has to share. She isn't married but has a younger and quite "buff" boyfriend. She doesn't have to boast; we've seen them together and he is immensely proud of her. They have fantastic chemistry that gives us all hope.

Christina, twenty-six, is recovering from her mastectomy three weeks ago and fears her boyfriend's averted glances. She feels weak for thinking of herself as having "diminished femininity," but honestly, that is precisely how she feels. She can't imagine his hand lovingly caressing a long red scar. Will he be mature enough to handle it?

Simone's fiancé quietly walked out of her life when she was diagnosed last August. We all try to console her that breast cancer holds a magnifying glass to issues that would have become visible later in the relationship, and she is lucky breast cancer saved her from more heartbreak in the long run. She holds her head high until she makes it, which I know she will.

Amidst the chatter, I wonder…can we hold these men – or ourselves, for that matter – accountable? As a media professional, I'm well attuned to the fact that we are bombarded by images of sexy push-up bras, cleavage, and silicone implants splashed all over the pages of women's magazines, the Academy Awards, and other media events that uphold impossible standards. Is a set of perfect breasts the icon of the feminine essence? Without them, will others subconsciously see us as less feminine?

The last group member silences the doubt in my rationally governed mind.

Evelyn.

Evelyn is thirty-one and has been married to her husband and college sweetheart, Leon, for seven years. She is a dancer with a long, lithe figure that reminds me of a graceful giraffe. Although I would not describe her as a vain woman, her physique is inextricably a part of who she is.

Evelyn described in unflinching detail the first time she took a shower after the bandages were removed from her bilateral mastectomy. She didn't expect to be overwhelmed by her emotions and wept alone in the shower for hours.

When Leon arrived home from work, he found her inconsolable and still in the shower. He climbed in his suit and dress shoes without missing a beat, as if he was saving her from drowning in the deep end of a pool. He held her in his arms and told her she had never looked more beautiful and she had become more of a woman than he could have imagined.

If that isn't one of the most touching, poignant, and simply poetic expressions of how love wins, well, I'm not sure what is.

Leon: 214 Cancer: Still 0.

Sunday, March 7th, 1999
Dear Journal, is what they say true? Should you never look back? Can you never really go back? …Will you suffer consequences if you do?

I'm reaching the end of "Journey of a Soul." I'm looking forward to leaving the past in the past, where it belongs.

In my last weeks in the Vortex known as Los Angeles, the final entry makes me laugh (with its ridiculousness). Our heroine (that would be me) is found obsessing about a refrigerator magnet. Yes, you heard me correctly. It was a small gift given to me by a friend who was being supportive when I was moving to LA.

The magnet had a folksy picture of a girl in a straw hat, a gingham shirt, and denim overalls walking down a dirt road approaching two divergent paths. A "New Direction" and "No Longer an Option," the signpost declares. The caption warned at the top of the magnet: "Never Look Back."

The day before, the movers would load all of my worldly possessions into a truck to return them from whence they came; I was making coffee in my little California kitchen when the magnet fell off the refrigerator door. The top portion that proclaimed "Never Look Back" broke off and ricocheted under the oven, never to be seen again.

I was convinced it was an ominous sign.

Perhaps that is why I got breast cancer: For defying the advice prescribed by a refrigerator magnet.

I've yet to come up with a better explanation.

Friday, March 12th
And, with that, Dear Journal, having (honestly) reached the (very final) end of the reflective journey and the span of my documented adult life with your siblings as my tour guide (Amen.) I've just cracked open Journal Four. "Full Circle." Not to fret! It is not water-stained or worn but young and crisp with the binder barely broken in, and the first *and sole entry (thankfully)* chronicles the day that the moving truck pulled up in front of the Blue House in Chicago and everything got "put back together" again.

Or so I thought.

As I stood in the frigid February air on the familiar front steps of the Blue House, supervising the movers dutifully carrying the boxes back into the same house they had left three years earlier, I noticed a small forlorn cardboard box forgotten in a snow bank.

The contents of the water-logged box?

The most precious possessions I own.

And *that* is how the worn and torn journals got their spots!

Saturday, March 13th, 1999
Oddly, as those boxes were making their way back into the Blue House, across the country back in the City of Angels that I had just forsaken, preparations were being made. Thousands of cancer specialists would be descending upon the Los

Angeles Convention Center for the thirty-fourth annual meeting of the American Society for Clinical Oncology in mid-May.

While I was settling back into my life with Brian in Chicago and, at long last, starting pre-natal consultation, Genentech was putting Dennis Slamon and my soon-to-be oncologist, Melody Cobleigh, on the stage at the ASCO meeting to talk about the results of the Herceptin clinical trials.

Melody would be honored to present the "649" results, phase three, for metastatic patients who had failed other treatments. According to Bazell's account, Melody had a touch of "stage fright" addressing such a large audience. Still, in her reserved and soft-spoken way, she "electrified" the crowd with indisputably thrilling results. The patients in these trials were generally regarded as "a graveyard," but Melody offered solid evidence that Herceptin could help women with severe metastatic breast cancer. Eight of 213 patients who completed the study had achieved a "complete pathological response." Meaning that the very fortunate 3.8% of their cancer disappeared entirely. Twenty-six or 12.2% had a partial response, with their tumors shrinking by fifty percent.

However, Dr. Cobleigh pointed out that the investigators themselves thought Herceptin was much better than that. She said the tumors did not shrink in at least thirty percent of the women, but *neither did they grow.* These women "officially" were not listed as benefiting from Herceptin but stable disease without progression for that population that should not be ignored. Melody further pointed out that among the women in the study whose cancer had failed to respond to "the biggest cannon of all, high-dose chemotherapy with bone marrow rescue," more than twenty-five percent benefited significantly from Herceptin. These responses were "especially gratifying." Melody spoke "heart to heart" to the clinicians, detailing data that proved the positive responses "occurred very rapidly." When Melody finished, it was clear the audience shared her enthusiasm.

The applause was "thunderous and sustained."

That evening, Genentech hosted cocktails under the stars at the Hollywood Terrace, at a Universal Studios lot in North Hollywood. The event was described as ... "A spectacularly clear evening ... the warm orange glow of the setting sun over the San Fernando Valley... setting the tone of the festivities... women's lives would be saved, and a huge fortune would be made."

Fortunes and lives inextricably intertwined.

That would be the future of cancer treatment.

Had I still lived in Los Angeles, I might have been annoyed by the gridlock on Wilshire Boulevard from the ASCO conference that night on my evening commute. Instead, I sit here in Chicago preparing for my upcoming surgery and the critical pathology results that will determine my fate. I can only cling to the infinite hope that I could be one of those elite responders, less than 4%, who become disease free.

Complete pathological response.

Even more than the symphonic phrase "no palpable mass," these three words could catapult me to the stars of breast cancer history.

Thirteen: Bald Karaoke

March 14th, 1999
A letter to my Grandmother,

Happy St. Patrick's Day! I've always associated this day with you and the "Luck of the Irish" card you would predictably send every March 17th, including the "green beer sponsorship."

The days are getting longer. It has been a long winter. My head is spinning! So much to do! Tomorrow is my final chemotherapy treatment. It's been a long, rocky road, but the end of the dark tunnel is in sight! I am going to request that they dye my Taxol green. Indeed, if they can dye the Chicago River, they can doctor my drugs for the celebration. Thursday morning, we depart for Ixtapa and Zihuantanejo, Mexico! Seven days of sand, sun, and surf! The pristine resort area of Ixtapa is a short cab ride to Zihuantanejo...a quaint fishing village. "Grittier" but lots to explore! Our hotel sits on cliffs overlooking the Pacific with a balcony and hammock for an all-important siesta. Catherine and Frank will make the sojourn to Chicago the weekend we return. I've got tickets to "Cirque Ingeniex." Catherine loves that big city sort of stuff.

I've been dialing up the days I spend at BBDO. I am looking forward to resuming a regular schedule. I was actually promoted while on leave of absence. I'll be managing a group of twelve with an expanded list of client responsibilities when I get back in the saddle.

Your current card is on my "Wall of Hope." Every card, letter and email I have received since last August hangs on ribbons tied to the staircase in our foyer. It is an impressive display of support.

By the way, I recently had the opportunity to help Gilda's Club (started by Gene Wilder) secure a major donation. Guess what? We got it!

The strength I've been blessed with I inherited from you, Grandmother.

Carpe Diem, Elizabeth.

Monday, March 15th
March Madness!

Philanthropic opportunities are coming out of the woodwork. Brian's employer and my first ad agency, Foote, Cone & Belding, has taken on "Y-Me."

Of all the not-for-profits in Chicago.

They are developing a legitimate advertising campaign, which includes the whole shebang: primary research/focus groups, top creative talent and a multi-media approach. FCB has a whole team working on the assignment, including planners, writers, art directors and media strategists. And, from what I've heard, they have locked up Matthew Rolston, recently known for his breakthrough GAP Khaki Swing commercials. Rolston was discovered by Andy Warhol back in the day. Pretty interesting choice for a breast cancer awareness campaign.

I'm impressed that FCB is throwing it's best at this, instead of treating it like a shoestring production, as is too often the case for pro-bono work.

Shannon and I were recruited to be part of a focus group this afternoon. About ten of us Y-Me members crammed into a little one-bedroom high-rise apartment to offer whatever insights the professionals might be able to unlock so they can boil it down to a "brief" so that people who know *nothing* about breast cancer will understand how to speak to people who do have breast cancer, in a provoking way.

The primary research began with us exercising our artistic skills, or lack thereof.

"Draw a picture of how you felt when you first learned of your diagnosis."

One woman, Mary, drew a tombstone. Sally drew a stick figure standing on a bridge, contemplating jumping off it. Shannon drew a picture of a cat sitting in a corner alone in an empty room. My illustration had a woman sitting alone on a raft in the middle of the ocean. Not a shoreline or even a seagull in sight.

"Now, illustrate how you felt after being connected with the resources at Y-Me."

I sketched a life preserver over the stick-figured woman, and added sea-worthy legs. I put a compass in her hands and a rescue boat approaching. I threw in a circle sun with little lines around it to represent hope. As an afterthought, I scribbled a thought bubble over the bald stick-figured head:

"I Will Survive!"

When the ladies from Foote Cone & Belding felt satisfied with what they got, they told us they would be doing a casting call for the campaign sometime in the late summer or fall. They would be using actual breast cancer fighters and survivors instead of models. They said they would be in touch to see if we would be willing to participate.

With a gray complexion and bald as a cue ball, I hardly feel like a face anyone would want to look at, let alone plaster on a billboard or place in a magazine. I laughed and responded while fanning myself with one hand like a southern debutante, feigning my best Georgian drawl.

"Why...me?"

Wednesday, March 17th, 1999

PROJECT: BETH - Status Report: A MILESTONE
I had my (hopefully) last chemotherapy infusion today and my LUCKY 13th Herceptin infusion.

"Can you dye my Taxol green?" I asked the nurses. They all laughed.

As I was leaving, the nurses hugged me and presented me with a t-shirt as a souvenir. The t-shirt has the hospital's logo and says, "RUSH Cancer Survivor, Carpe Diem." I suggested they print up a new batch with something bolder, like, "I went through six months of chemotherapy, and all I got was this lousy t-shirt."

They all laughed again.

It felt strange. The nurses, that room, the other patients and the weekly routine has been my life for the past seven months. I felt a little bit like a released prisoner might feel. Wondering, will I survive on the "outside?" Saying "goodbye" felt forced and inappropriate. After all, according to those annoying statistics, I could be back "in the char" in less than a year.

On a lighter note, I sent my Grandmother Virginia flowers for St. Patrick's Day this morning.

Red tulips, of course. It seemed fitting.

Monday, March 29th, 1999

The day after my last chemotherapy treatment, we boarded a plane and left cancer in Chicago.

Mexico.

Honestly, I only thought about cancer twice. Well, okay, three times.

The first time I took my straw hat off to go swimming, I became conscious of some other guests taking notice of my bald head.

The second time, when I was horseback riding on the beach. The experience was so beautiful; I said a silent thank you to the Universe and acknowledged that cancer allowed me to be fully in that moment.

And the third time was over a romantic candlelight dinner on the cliffs. I had packed some artificial eyelashes and thought I'd try them for a special occasion. I wanted to feel beautiful just for one night. I was mortified when one of them fell off my eyelid onto the table. The waiter thought it was a centipede and tried to kill it.

Tuesday, March 30th
Coming back home could have been a big thump. But it wasn't. The next day, Cathy and Frank arrived. Cirque Ingeniux, Cafe Iberico, Shamrock Shuffle 8k, Soul Kitchen. It was a whirlwind of activity.

Today the temps hit 70 degrees. Sunny. Daffodils. Six days away from surgery.

A letter arrived today. A bit tattered as it had been returned to the sender for a zip code. It was initially postmarked on March 17th from Gaylord, Michigan. The penmanship is a bit jagged, a labor of love from a woman who no longer has steady hands to write.

"Tulips on St. Patrick's Day. Oh my."

Wednesday, March 31st
Today, I decided to call my grandmother.

We Distels are known as "great communicators," and I mean that facetiously. Aside from the more regular conversation we've been having since my diagnosis, an actual call to a family member generally means that someone was born, sick or dying.

It's like we have a way of communicating without communicating.

As I waited for Natie to fetch my grandmother and help her to the phone, it struck me: granddaughter and grandmother, facing their mortality together. On many levels, that was part of the exceptional bond we had been sharing over the past several months.

I excitedly shared the excellent news about the "gratifying response" I had to the untested protocol and all the research and reading I had done on Herceptin. How fascinating it was and how she should read "Her-2," I'd be happy to send her a copy…and how ready I was for the surgery…and she doesn't need to worry about me, not one bit.

What I really wanted to tell her *was that I loved her.*

But I didn't get the chance.

I realized she was tired, heard all she needed to hear, and was content that I was okay. And before Natie put the phone back on its cradle, I could hear her say aloud as she was being helped back to her room, "That's my girl."

That's all I needed to hear from the woman who says so much by saying so little.

Just like a great quote.

Monday, April 5th
It has been three weeks since my final chemotherapy, and I'm regaining my strength.

So much so that I thought I would be up for a "last hurrah" for my right breast. I had the perfect plan for Saturday night involving Maria and "Cake." Two tickets to a concert at The Rivera, a rundown, once-stately but hip theater in sketchy Uptown, were sitting on my pine desk, waiting to be taken out for a night on the town.

I've been listening to alternative rock as a welcome break from bawling my eyes out over classical music. I've been taken by their sarcastic lyrics since their third album, "Prolong the Magic," was released.

Who better to celebrate with than another survivor who's made the same sacrifice to save her own life? Maria seemed like an excellent choice, but she explained that she wasn't allowed to go to places where they served alcohol because of her religious beliefs and strict Muslim practices. However, she could make just this one exception.

Kind of like Allah gave her a "mulligan" because of the whole cancer thing.

I gave the false eyelashes another chance. I chose a white lace t-shirt with my best push-up bra and encouraged Maria to wear her new wig and vamp it up, introducing her to the miracles of make-up. Black bob, smoky eyes and dramatic liner.

Maria looked like a Moroccan Marilyn Monroe.

Before the doors opened, I coerced my starlet sidekick into enjoying a poetry slam at the infamous Green Mill. "Would you ladies like a couple of our famous dirty martinis?" We exchanged tentative glances that said, "we couldn't, could we?" Allah giving Maria a mulligan is one thing, but this is another.

Well, one thing led to another, as it often can, and before I knew it, we were enjoying a second or was it a third martini? Not wanting to offend our good natured and attentive bartender who was shaking them so perfectly. Our minds seemed to have a mind of their own. Like a pair of breast cancer outlaws, we went from feeling no pain to insanely invincible.

I remember bits and pieces of the evening as if it were an esoteric music video. But, whatever we wouldn't or shouldn't have done, the moment that will always be vivid and clear is when Maria and I worked our way to the edge of the stage, dancing and swaying to "Never There." Caught in a wave of freedom and sweat, we exchanged suggestive smiles and peeled off our "camouflage" to publicly reveal our beautiful bald heads. The accepting strangers around us cheered as if Maria and I were part of the band.

Maria and I polished off the evening performing bald karaoke in an Uptown dive bar, playing tribute to Gloria Gaynor and Helen Reddy. She didn't know the words, and I couldn't carry a tune to save my life, but no one seemed to care.

Now that, my friend, is what it means to "Live W I D E."

"Better to live one day as a lion than
for a thousand years as a sheep."

~ *Tibetan Proverb or Mussolini*

Sunday, April 11th
On Brian's 37th birthday, Thursday, April 8th, I woke up a 4:58 AM. I would have given anything to stay in bed, insulated from the IVs and scalpels that awaited.

At 8:51 am, I walked into Rush St. Luke's Medical Center with my right breast for the last time.

Packed in my overnight bag was my pink Y-Me Survivor's cap, my journal with the card from the 20-year survivor tucked inside the cover and the little pewter box inscribed: "Tutt E Possible."

"Aunt Beth, you sit in the waiting chair," my now four-year-old niece Kelsey ordered as the group of us fumbled around in the registration area, "and you will see the doctor, and then you will have a rest, and then it will be OK!" Such strength and reassurance from a four-year-old made me believe that perhaps that Hollywood ending was waiting for me right down the hospital corridor.

I was ushered into a changing room and handed another awkward gown, disposable slippers and a plastic bag to put my belongings in. As I pulled off my t-shirt, I was struck with finality. The "skin and tissue I can live without" would soon be gone; a long red scar would be left in its place. I felt like I was sending my old friend, my right breast, off to the death chamber. "I'll never forget you," I whispered.

"Miss Distel-Grady?" The Impatient Surgical Assistant shattered my moment of respect.

As the anesthesia kicked in, the Sensitive Surgeon leaned over the gurney. "One laaaast inssssspeeeection...," he slurred as he made a green "X" on my right breast, and I succumbed to a drug-induced bliss, smiling because they marked the correct breast...my toes went stone cold...bright lights and shiny things danced over my head...I squinted and deliberately conjured up a comforting sequence of grainy snippets from my past, like a movie trailer...girls yodeling...a blue dress blowing over Lake Michigan...bells ringing and a thud, as a grand old mulberry tree collapses.

Five hours later, I woke up.

My right side hurt.

Now, I thought might sanitize the first night after the surgery out of this journal because I didn't want to relive it. Ever again. It honestly absolutely positively sucked.

Brian offered to stay overnight, but he looked so exhausted and spent. I sent him back to the Blue House with the rest of the family. He kissed me on the forehead ever-so-gently and then seemed to dissolve into thin air.

I tried to remember what the nurse said about the IV-fed pain medication... morphine, press the button, blah, blah, every 30 minutes. As the anesthesia began to wear off, I became more and more aware of the burning pain I would later rate 15 on a scale of 1 to 10.

It felt like they had removed my breast and underarm, stretched the skin they could spare as tight as a drum over the giant gaping hole, and stapled it shut. And if that wasn't enough, it felt like a serpent had burrowed under my skin and was trying to claw his way out. I was sure the surgery angered the remaining cancer cells; they were now drug-and-knife-resistant and spreading like a brush fire in the Santa Anna winds. It hurt so much I thought I might pass out, and I started pushing the morphine button like a monkey every ten seconds, hoping either I would OD or a rush of warm relief would wash over me, but it did not. I feel wet and sticky and look down in horror to see my bedsheets covered in bright red blood. I start screaming for a nurse, who won't come. No one can hear me.

After all, I've been through, what a way to go.

I imagine my somber family gathered in the doctor's office tomorrow morning. The bad news is that she hemorrhaged to death because a vein burst when she couldn't get her pain medication. The good news is that the pathology was clean. The therapy was effective.

She died cancer-free.

When a haggard, over-worked nurse finally answers the page –about three in the morning and after I've been writhing in pain since midnight – she explains I'm not hemorrhaging. The drains from my surgical site and the bag collecting the fluid overflow. She will change the sheets if I can sit up. I tell her she is insane, which doesn't help the situation. She says she will send in someone to check the morphine IV when I tell her that is fucked up too, and then she leaves me alone in my bloodbath to reflect on how far bad manners will get you during the graveyard shift. Still, I didn't feel remorse, and then a male nurse came and checked the IV and confirmed it was crimped or some other bullshit, so I wasn't getting the morphine. Now it will work, and I press the button like I'm setting off a nuclear bomb to end the world, which I almost wish I could, but then I think of all the innocents and decide I didn't mean that and now the pain…killer…starts… to…kick…in.

I woke an hour later and felt like I might vomit, then THE PAIN…I press the button, and one type of pain goes away, but another returns, like a snake head, and this pain isn't just local…it feels like my entire body is covered with red biting ants. I page the nurse; she calls a doctor who determines I'm allergic to morphine and asks if I would like some Tylenol instead.

That's when I began to plot my escape.

I sat up before I felt like I could. And got out of bed before I thought I could. And walked to the bathroom because it was the only place I had to go. I convinced the nurses to take off the compression stockings. I reached my right arm above my head and touched myself to understand what was happening underneath those bandages. Knowing what was no longer under there.

I put on lipstick, blush, and contacts, drew in my eyebrows, and donned my pink survivor's baseball cap to impress everyone with how stunning I looked.

"I'll be checking out this morning," I told the nurses on Saturday morning. "The doctor says I'm roadworthy."

'The nurses think I'm ready to be released," I told the doctor.

I packed and waited, fully dressed by nine a.m., sitting on the edge of my bed like a kid going home from summer camp. They brought a wheelchair, and I said goodbye. My father waited at the front entrance in the car. "Can I do that again?" I asked. I hoped with all my heart that I would never have to.

My pathology results are promised by next Tuesday.

I envision my poor right breast sitting in a jar like a science experiment next to a rattlesnake or a frog, stewing in florescent formaldehyde. And for the first time, I wondered what they do with the "Skin and Tissue I Can Live Without." I imagine they incinerate it. Perhaps I should have asked for the ashes to keep in a pink urn, or to spread the remains over Lake Michigan during Breast Cancer Awareness month.

Nonetheless.

Whatever my breast's fate will be or was, the pathology results are critical and will provide the roadmap for the next course of treatment. As "gratifying" as my response to the Herceptin appeared to be to the touch, any remaining cancer cells or positive lymph nodes means this isn't the finish line but the beginning of a new marathon.

Regardless of how this all plays out, I am ready.

The lessons I have learned in the past seven months, the people I have met, and the courage I have seen have renewed my belief in that which is inextinguishable.

Sharon is going to travel the world and LIVE until she dies ... Judy is taking tango lessons at age 72 and is still as in love with her departed husband as the day she married him ... Pat has traveled to every cancer treatment center in the country to find that one single doctor who might be able to save flamingo Grace…Maria prays on her knees every day for her safe and healthy return to Morocco to her husband and son…Leon made Evelyn feel even more like a woman after her bilateral mastectomy…Anne fought breast cancer recurrences for two decades and completed the Herceptin trials…Lilian lost the love of her life to a 23-year battle with cancer and has become a great philanthropist, making a difference in the treatments available to other patients.

"The human spirit is stronger than
anything that can happen to it."
– CC Scott.

You see, it is pretty simple. I have already won my battle with cancer.

Fourteen: No More Tears

Monday, April 12th

It feels like the world is again holding its breath with me, waiting for the pathology. I've tried calling several times with various effects and accents, posing as an intern, a nurse, and a clinician gathering statistics for a research project, as if that were even remotely possible. I got put through to oncology and bounced around a few times without success. It could be two more days before the report is back from the lab.

Needless to say, ...

IT

IS

A

VERY

LONG

NIGHT.

Tuesday, April 13th

Terrified we all might shatter into a million pieces if we didn't hear the lab results today, I continued with my unorthodox measures - this time calling precisely at noon when I thought I might get someone new covering a lunch shift. Mom and I were huddled in our pajamas together in the pink guest bedroom, bracing ourselves as I dialed the phone. I got through to an affable lab technician with whom I was evidently confusing and convincing enough to cause him to read my pathology results directly to me.

As the technician sprayed me with medical jargon, the phone slipped from my hand and dropped to the floor...

Mom, hanging on every muffled word, is looking at me, the moment so infinitely fragile, one word would change the world as we know it... her eyes brimming with tears preparing for the worst...

I took every bit of strength I have left to relay the results to her.

"Complete Pathological Response."

That's right.

No microscopic evidence that I ever had breast cancer.

The two of us exhaled, and in that breath, we let go... of the anxiety, despair, and fear we had carried so bravely for the past seven months. We sat embracing each other, not speaking a word, for at least an hour or two or three. Who knows. We filled the room with tears of gratitude, disbelief, relief... and emotions I never knew I could feel.

I know the probability of the results I was incredibly fortunate to receive.

But the odds mean nothing to me anymore.

The odds are no match for the Universe CEO, who had been listening all along.

ELIZABETH: 317, Cancer: 0

Saturday, April 17th

The Blue House is still. Mom went back to Michigan this morning. She has a life to get back to.

As do I.

212

The phone has stopped ringing off the hook, and I'm trying my best to process the blur of the past eight months. Most of the "get well" flower arrangements are fading and will soon make their way to the garbage. The flood of cards, letters, and congratulatory e-mails is trickling off.

Outside, it's sunny. High 60s today.

I did it.

I made it to Spring.

> **"She turned to the sunlight and shook her yellow head.**
> **And whispered to the Universe: Winter is Dead."**
>
> **~A.A. Milne**

Tuesday, April 20th

I still have thirteen weeks of radiation therapy, continued infusions of my miracle drug, Herceptin, and reconstruction ahead of me.

But deal with it all, I gladly will.

I've found a cosmetic surgeon, one of the best, willing to take me as a client, although his practice is decidedly elective breast augmentation. When asked what "result" I sought in the consult, I replied, without missing a beat, that I wanted to look 22 again, please. I've more than earned a matching set of permanently youthful breasts. The "process" is long, with tissue expansion before the radiation begins, then suspended, and then resumed when my skin is pliable. The right breast gets an implant, and the left gets a "lift," ending with an areola tattoo. I lived on the border of Venice Beach as a transplanted, roller-blading, blond divorcee and managed to evade even a tasteful tattoo. Still, I'm happy to surrender my tattoo virginity for this.

Making Beth 22 again will take about nine months.

Aside from all that excitement, I will return to work in five days, resuming everyday life again. But, as it's been said, "Normal" isn't quite as "Normal" as it once seemed.

> *"I can't go back to yesterday,*
> *Because I was a different person then."*
>
> ~ Lewis Carroll

Also, I threw the Purple Pajamas away.

Monday, April 26th
Dear Grandmother,

I spent the entire day gardening yesterday. I have always loved spring, which is even more special this year.

I went back to work today. I have promised myself to take your advice, "slow down," and respect my own "boundaries" now. After all, it is just Advertising. I remind myself.

I'm starting my radiation therapy. I pick up my friend Maria (from Casablanca) and take her to the center daily. Maria will be "going home" in a few weeks. I am planning to visit her in Morocco, hopefully, to include Paris and some of Spain, this fall.

I have been helping my friend Shannon with a speech for her colleagues. She had a recurrence, and we don't know the prognosis. We have become very close. She is an accomplished and articulate woman I am honored to have as a friend. You would approve.

By the way, I know you won't take offense because you appreciate a sharp wit, but I will never experience the rewards of a long life by seeing my "tits in my shoes," as you put it last Christmas. I've consulted with a plastic surgeon who promised he could give me a permanently youthful result. I think I've earned it.

If I am privileged enough to celebrate five years of good health and it looks like my story will have a happy ending, I promise to write a book about this journey and dedicate it to you, Grandmother.

Carpe Diem and Tutto E Possible,

Elizabeth

Friday, April 30th
My first week back at BBDO went pretty well. It's funny that all the things I pursued fiercely "B.C." don't matter anymore.

"What Happiness Is Not"
A corner office, an impressive title, and a six-figure salary.

A perfect body. Having all the answers.

A broad group of acquaintances you think are your friends.

A checklist of all the conventional things you thought your life should include.

~ My Enlightened After-Cancer Self

By the way, today I told my "story" to a woman who was just diagnosed after she told me she thought her chances of survival were about 1%. "Always put yourself in that top percent. Someone gets to be that 1%; why not you?" My words gave her great hope, and that made me genuinely happy.

So, I may not have solved the meaning of life, but I have learned a few things.

Sunday, May 2nd
Dearest Journal, Hey... How are you? My eyelashes are starting to fill in again, and my eyebrows are, too. Today, I began to scour the cabinets for the toiletries I had packed away last November, but then I decided I should treat myself to a Walgreens shopping spree. I forgot how many decisions are at stake! Extra volume or extra-moisturizing, color-protection, a side of aloe for sensitive skin? The lady at the checkout thought I had gone mad when it totaled $127.61 for hair and shaving products, mainly because I still don't have much hair. I collected my favorite CDs, cranked up Santana as loud as I could and sang at the top of my lungs. And the special bottle of shampoo I ultimately decided to use? Why? None other than Johnson & Johnson's Baby Shampoo, of course. After all, as the bottle itself and one iconic advertising campaign proclaim:

"No More Tears."

(Improved Formula, Now with No Formaldehyde.)

Friday, May 7th
Speaking of tears…

Instead of crying once a day, I've decided that I am going to do something incredibly outrageous and just plain silly.

Today, I walked down Michigan Avenue in one of my best Ann Taylor suits, *barefoot.*

And you know what? Not one person noticed. And, even though it was a little cold to be out and about without any shoes, I skipped along the sea of serious passers-by, whom all seemed to be both rushing and sleepwalking through life at the same time. I smiled, cherishing the lessons I have learned over the past eight months.

> "There is not one shred of evidence that life
> is meant to be taken too seriously."
>
> ~ Kelsey Virginia Taylor

Sunday, May 23rd, 12:07 pm
Dear Journal, I'm not quite sure how to say this so that I will come out with it...

I am going to start a new journal.

Today.

And as I embrace another "new beginning," I realize, that your 1st page is still a blank slate.

After everything we've been through together, we need a suitable title!

How about, "Dance with the Dragon." No. Too much like that Kevin Costner movie..."Project Beth" would be an apt choice, but alas, not enough gravitas. Hmmmmm. "Sailing in Uncharted Water" sounds a bit maritime-ish. If we want to go the humorous route, "Reflections in Bald Karaoke and the Meaning of Life" could be a frothy title kept in good company by so many other tongue-in-cheek gutsy cancer memoirs as of late ... or, if you'd prefer, we amplify the medical significance, "Her Story," and pay homage to the benevolent drug Herceptin, which I was so incredibly fortunate to receive. On the other hand, given the story of love and loyalty that underlies it all, "The Bride Wore Brown" could be an interesting slant. Or we could just call a spade a spade: "Cancer Sucks for Clairol and a Lot of Folks." Cathartic but too irreverent.

(Deep breath.) That was tedious. But wait. It's so obvious. And right in front of me.

"L i v e   W   I   D   E"

And with that, my faithful friend and confidant, I'll bid you farewell with two quotes. One of my own, as a reminder of what we intuitively know but chronically fail to put into practice. The concept of Carpe Diem can start anytime:

"No one can promise you will live long.

So

L i v e   W   I   D   E."

- Elizabeth Mary Catherine

...And the second?

Well, the second is to remind me that whatever the meaning of this life is - or isn't - the best we can do is to reveal its ambiguity. Life doesn't unfold predictably...

"I wanted a perfect ending.
Now I've learned the hard way,
some poems don't rhyme
And some stories don't have a clear
beginning, middle and end."
- Gilda Radner

And with that, my dearest friend, you will take your place in a special box where I've packed away all the cards and letters from the past eight months.

Except one.

The card from early November, from the 20-year survivor, with the brave ballet dancer that embodies grace, agility, determination, and perseverance.

"Those who hear not the music think the dancer mad."

I promise myself I will *never* stop listening to the music and I will live *every day* knowing there is no guarantee of *anything.*

Regardless of how the rest of my story unfolds.

Post Script

When the FDA approved Herceptin in 1998, the long-term survival rates attributable to the antibody were entirely unknown. Elizabeth celebrated her 25th anniversary on St. Patrick's Day 2023 and considers it a great privilege to be a long-term survivor of Her2 positive Inflammatory Breast Cancer.

Elizabeth has been honored to participate in fundraising and speaking events for Gilda's Club, American Cancer Society, 3-Day Walk, Susan G. the Komen and other NFP's. She was featured in a Y-Me campaign titled "I Will Survive." She has also served as a mentor for Imerman Angels, where she received "Rock Star" status.

It took much longer than she would have liked to publish her journal as a proper Thank You. In 2016 she took "Live W I D E" over the finish line as an unpublished manuscript. Little did she know what the Universe still had in store, referred to in her *second book* as the "Post-Cancer Apocalypse." It took another seven years to publish this book *commercially.*

Shortly after Elizabeth's recovery, her Grandmother announced one evening, "I'm becoming a grumpy old lady. I don't want to be a grumpy old lady." Virginia passed away peacefully in her sleep that night. Every card and letter Elizabeth sent her was found carefully preserved in Virginia's dresser drawer.

Maria had a favorable response to chemotherapy and returned to Morocco. A year later, she had a recurrence and returned to the United States for more treatment. Elizabeth and Maria fell out of touch. Elizabeth hopes that someday Maria will find this book and remember the night they threw their wigs in the air.

Shannon managed her disease and lived another seven years with metastatic Inflammatory Breast Cancer and her mantra, "I just want to live until I die." And she did exactly that, remarried just months before her time with us ended. She left a legacy of dignity, courage and grace. Her last painting hangs at the University of Notre Dame.

Following Elizabeth's complete response to Herceptin and chemotherapy, the clinical trial began replicating the untested protocol she had received, eventually becoming the standard care for advanced-stage HER2-positive breast cancer. To this day, Dr. Melody Cobleigh refers to Herceptin as "the most rewarding experience of my life in medicine."

In 2006, the FDA approved it for use in early-stage HER2-positive breast cancer. Since 1998, Herceptin has treated millions of patients worldwide. Herceptin remains one of the most revolutionary and significant cancer treatment breakthroughs in the past two decades.

The legacy of all those connected with the development of Herceptin, especially the brave women who made the ultimate sacrifice to complete the clinical trials, lives on as a testament to the triumph of the human spirit over adversity.

Ten years after surviving Inflammatory Breast Cancer, Elizabeth did get an adorable dog. She named him, "Spots!," after her journals.

Gratitude and Acknowledgements

Dr. Melody Cobleigh and Team at Rush-Presbyterian-St. Luke's. You were believers in a better therapy and on the tip of the spear for a breakthrough in breast cancer treatment. I am eternally grateful for all the years I had to write this book. You added immeasurable width and length to my life.

Dr. Dennis Slamon. For Standing Up to Cancer in a BIG Way. Thanks to the twelve years you and your colleagues conducted the research leading to the development of Herceptin, I am among the thousands of lives that have been made longer by your commitment to a cure. Thank you for prevailing against the maze of institutional hurdles. Without your dedication, there would be no book.

Lillian Tartikoff. You are Living Proof that philanthropic efforts in the crusade against cancer can make a difference. The influence you had on the Herceptin clinical trials saved my life. I am just one of so many indebted to your selfless efforts. Thank you for making the world a more beautiful place.

Lisa Paulsen. Galvanizer of the Human Spirit. You helped Hollywood fund research for more technologically advanced treatments for Cancer. Thank you for bringing a sense of urgency we desperately need in the crusade against cancer.

Brian Patrick Grady. The only man strong enough to put up with me. Twice. I love you more than words can say. For your unwavering optimism and enthusiasm, never failing to make me laugh, being an Oak when I needed one and never, ever giving up on me... You are a Prince among men. And, Brian Patrick, I would do it all over again... (throwing in a few edits that we both deserve). Regardless of our circumstances, I will be by your side forever. (Insert thumbs up here.)

Nancy Grady. You will always be a mother to me. You sat with me through every treatment and doctor visit and kept a positive outlook no matter what. You were my rudder in the eye of the storm. You have friends in high places. Of that, I'm sure.

Pat Rodbro. Pat, you were my "beacon" during the darkest days. Your encouragement meant more to me than you know. I've done my best to be a "Pat" to others.

Genentech and other investigators. The Genentech team of scientists, including Len Presta, Paul Carter, Michael Shepard Axel Ullrich, Art Levinson, and countless others whose names and contributions might not ever be celebrated and honored in the way they deserve. And to the company's leadership, thank you for having the moral conscience to do the right things ultimately.

Gilda's Club Chicago. Thank you for giving us a haven during my treatment. I said it in my speech... Gilda's Club is an assembly of courageous people that feels like home.

Jonny Imerman & Imerman Angels! The energy and creativity you've infused into the lives of those affected by cancer is a breath of fresh air! Your unique matching program understands those who have the lived experience are an invaluable resource. Thanks for all the advocacy, events, mentoring programs, fund-raising and inspiration you and your organization provide. All of you at IA are ROCK STARS in my book!

FBC. For your brilliant and beautiful work on the pro-bono campaign, "I Will Survive." Thank you for using your creative force for good! And for giving me my big break in Advertising. You never forget your first.

George McAndrews. The Irish attorney I secured in an elevator pitch. Literally. Thank goodness your firm is on the 34th floor. Thank you for seeing something worth supporting in me. Go, Irish!

Kurt Beeken and George at Henry David Clothiers in Chicago. For your southern hospitality and for allowing us to shoot our video trailer in your high-end and beautiful store on Clinton Street in the city of big shoulders.

Ana Miyares. The photo queen extraordinaire. You were the first person to offer to help me with this book (the Irish attorney was number 2). Your generosity and belief in me and my dreams meant a great deal. Gracias.

"Pam." The 20-year survivor I never had the honor of meeting who sent me the card with the "mad dancer." Pam, I don't even know your last name or where you are today, but the space you have occupied in my life is immense. Thank you for inspiring me to open my ears and LISTEN to the music with all of my heart.

Last of all but certainly not least: Me. Thank you for believing in your dreams, Elizabeth. Keep holding your standards high. And pay no attention to those who gossip and throw stones at you. But, Elizabeth, you really need to work on your punctuality!

My Farewell Letter

(To read at the celebration of my Life...if I didn't make it across the finish line.)

To The People I Love -

My time here wasn't as long as I would have liked, but it was wider than I could have imagined. I could fill the Great Lakes with the things I could say to all of you, but for once, in my overly articulate life (if I can still use the present tense), I'm going to be succinct.

Facing the end of my life wasn't sad.

I experienced an awakening and a sharpening of my thoughts and senses that words can't describe. I felt things so deeply and profoundly... the smallest of things would move me to tears...not tears of great sadness, but of being overwhelmed by life's magnificence.

Someday, you will understand.

Please don't wait for a crisis to live a more aware and grateful life. For, as it has been said:

> *"The tragedy of life is not death, but what we let die inside us while we live."*

Death is inevitable; the variable is how we choose to live.

Here are a few simple suggestions from the vantage point of someone – that would be me – who was "involuntarily enlightened."

Please don't assume that you will have an unlimited supply of years here to realize your dreams. Banish the phrase "one of these days." And, while you're at it...stop saving things for a "special occasion." Every day is a special occasion.

Don't miss the opportunity to tell the people that matter to you how you feel about them. Turn to the person standing next to you, right this second, and...Tell Them, Damn It!

Don't be sad for long. Crying is mandatory today. But, after you've taken the time you need to adjust to the fact that I'm no longer here physically, I hope you will smile and laugh often when you think of me. I know I've given you all a sufficient amount of amusing material to work with. As it has been said, people are never really gone until they are forgotten. Don't you dare let me become transient!

And, if I may add just one last thing...and I suppose I can, because it is my funeral after all, and who in their right mind is going to interrupt the guest of honor putting in her final two cents?

Of all the things I learned from facing my mortality, the most crucial lesson is as true and clear as a full moon piercing the night sky.

There is ONE thing that nothing in this life can suppress. Not cancer, not even death.

In the end, LOVE is the *only thing that matters*.

That much, I'm sure of.

Now, thankfully we are finished with the sentimental portion of the day.

I expect you all to eat and drink like no one is counting, dance like no one is watching and outdo one another with stories of "Remember when..."

Make me proud of my legacy.

L I V E   W I   D   E   today and every day that you are given.

Elizabeth Mary Catherine
Cancer Warrior
December 7th, 1961 ~ TBD

Symbolism

The Snow Angel. The Snow Angel represents the daughter she longed for, which she will never have.

Red Tulips. Red tulips symbolize the belief in "spring" and eternal love. That one was obvious.

The Mulberry Tree. The Old Mulberry tree has lived a long life and weathered many winters and, while still magnificent to behold, is slowly deteriorating and nearing the end of her life, perhaps seemingly symbolic of the author's grandmother. However, the author's melancholy relationship with the tree is less obvious. In her poem, she wistfully romanticizes the long life of fulfillment the tree has enjoyed. She bore fruit. She had deep roots. She was content in one place. She didn't have to forage or seek water or sun. The Mulberry Tree had the existence the author herself longed for.

Symphony of Sorrowful Songs Three movements were composed by Henryk Gorecki in Poland between October and December 1976. A 15th century Polish lament. The second movement is a message written on the wall of a Gestapo cell during World War II. The dominant themes of the symphony are separation through war. The second book in the trilogy reveals why this symphony is so profoundly meaningful to the author.

Owls. The Owls represent wisdom and intuition, which she ascribes to her grandmother and oncologist, Dr. Cobleigh. In literature, The Owl can symbolize gaining clarity in the darkness, the introspective journey the author is thrust into.

Children's Books. Storytelling became a coping mechanism for the author. References to books from her childhood, littered throughout the journals, like a trail of breadcrumbs…But where is it leading us? Again, book number two.

Vortex. Negative vortices spin in a counter-clockwise motion, exerting a pull on the energy in your body, draining it of vitality. The author's experience in LA was the counter-clockwise motion that returned the author to her past, preventing her from embracing the "new beginning" she had hoped for. The author respects the fine residents of Los Angeles and the great state of California and genuinely means no offense. It was the experience and perception she had at the time.

Mocking Moon. The moon on her journal cover symbolizes that elusive something that haunts the author and many of us.

Hollywood. References began from her original journal while living in Los Angeles. They are amplified in the book because, ultimately and ironically, Hollywood came to her rescue and saved her life. Thanks to Revlon's donation, the EIF grant, and other generous donations, the FDA approval of Herceptin was accelerated, making the benevolent drug available when Elizabeth needed it.

Black Daisies. Daisies are a metaphor for a married woman, of course. But also, when stained black in the center, it represents the loss of innocence. The author did not realize why the idea of Black Daisies kept surfacing as she wrote, seemingly coming from a deep place. "Expansive fields of Black Daisies" is revealed in the second book, "Unbreakable Girl," to represent the shocking pervasiveness of childhood sexual abuse. The second book reveals clinical studies linking childhood abuse to physical and mental conditions, including anorexia, PTSD, anxiety, depression, alcohol abuse and cancer as an adult.

Negotiating With the Universe from the Bathroom Floor. After completing her 1st book and immersing herself in available research on childhood trauma, she understands why her book begins here. Most intrafamilial CSA occurs in the bathroom. This sensitive subject is explored with integrity, not in graphic terms, in Unbreakable Girl, in which the author must come to terms with her unthinkable past at long last.

Dance With Your Heart
Your Feet Will Follow

Lesser-Known Symptoms & Signs

The best way to minimize your chances of being diagnosed with advanced-stage breast cancer is to be disciplined about your self-exams and immediately report any unusual changes to your doctor. This is the behavior associated with early detection, which is the key to effective treatment and survival if you are diagnosed.

Lumps are far from the only symptom of which you should be aware. Here are eight more symptoms and signs indicative of breast cancer

1. An unusual rash, especially around the nipple.
2. Sudden increase or decrease in size to either or both breasts.
3. A swollen lymph node in your armpit or by your collarbone.
4. Strange discharge from your nipple without squeezing it.
5. Pain in your breast or armpit that's constant.
6. Skin texture suddenly feels like a puckered orange peel or dimply.
7. A nipple that changes direction or suddenly becomes inverted.
8. An area of thickened or lumpy breast tissue.

NOTE: The author's diagnosis of Inflammatory Breast Cancer is a rare form of breast cancer, representing approximately 1-3% of all breast cancer diagnoses. Other breast cancers may include similar terms, such as "infiltrating breast cancer," "invasive breast cancer," or "in situ breast cancer." These may be abbreviated as "ibc," but are not the same as IBC or Inflammatory Breast Cancer. If you know someone who has been described as having ibc/IBC, you should not assume that the information in this book applies to their symptoms, treatment, or prognosis.

"Bird on a Tree"

[Painting by Shannon 2004]

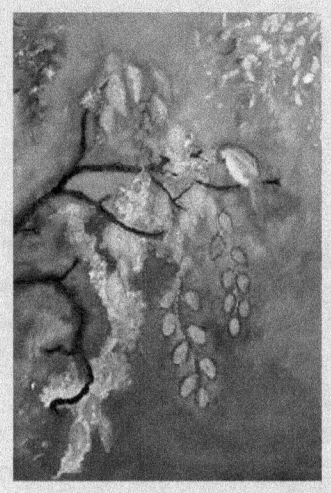

"Her painting is a delicate whisper.
A voice is searching for its universal chorus."

My Overdue Letter of Gratitude

March 17th, 2016

Dr. Melody Cobleigh

Rush Presbyterian St. Luke's Medical Center

I made a promise many years ago that - if I lived to tell it - I would write a book as an act of gratitude to those connected with what I believed to be a remarkable medical odyssey.

I remember, as if yesterday, hearing the breaking news about the FDA approval of Herceptin. I had just been diagnosed with inflammatory breast cancer. I was sitting in the waiting of a medical institution, floating adrift without a rudder or any idea of where to turn next.

Somehow, I navigated my way to you and the good people at Rush Presbyterian St. Luke's.

Melody, because you were a believer in a better therapy and on the tip of the spear for a true breakthrough in breast cancer treatment, this St. Patrick's Day, I am celebrating my 17th anniversary of "perfect health."

As my next level of gratitude, I (eventually) plan to take this book forward to a published form. While a neophyte to publishing, I realize that patient/doctor confidentiality may require some creative edits, which I am prepared to do. In that version, "Dr. Save-the-Day" might appear instead of you. This "inside edition" - my unpublished manuscript - is meant for your eyes and to share with whomever you choose. Consent is a bridge I will cross another day. Today is about saying Thank You in my own way.

In the years since its approval, Herceptin may have faded as a lead news story, headline, or top-selling book, but its legacy lives on in the years it has given to many women, including myself.

"Live WIDE" does not pretend to pose as a medically precise or Pulitzer-winning work of art. It decidedly is a gift from my heart. And while I can never repay you for the length and width, you added to my life, I hope you will accept my unforgivably belated and humble attempt.

Simply said, Melody, thank you for saving my life.

Elizabeth Distel

The "After Cancer Dance"

"I can't go back to yesterday because I was a different person then."

Lewis Carroll

The "AC" or "After Cancer" period represents a unique odyssey itself.

The familiarity and routine of the treatment program comes to an abrupt end. Phone calls, email cards, words of encouragement and support groups trickle away.

Like a catch and release program, the patient is cast back into the wild, expected to integrate into normal life. All assume the survivor has survived. But "normal" isn't as "normal" as it once seemed.

"You can't club a fish over the head, throw it back in the water and expect it to swim again," I tried to explain. But no one was listening.

Adding fuel to the flames, the possibility of recurrence lingers like a dragon lying in wait at the end of the tunnel. Or so it seems to a survivor, watching support members experience recurrences, become metastatic, move into hospice and eventually run out of medical options.

This was the leg of the journey where I lost my footing and stumbled.

I was drowning, but noone understood my struggle.

My career suffered nearly irreparable damage and my marriage dissolved for a second time. I took a sabbatical and moved back to Northern Michigan, where I spent time with my sister Catherine living on a small lake. I would spend all day floating in a canoe, watching the clouds go by. During this time, I practiced being "still," heeding the last words of advice from my grandmother ... "Elizabeth, slow down. If I knew then what I know now."

Take time to be still today.

See what the Universe has to say.

Herceptin (Trastuzumab) Development: Key Milestones

1975: Georges Kohler and Cesar Milstein, scientists at the Medical Research Council. Laboratory of Molecular Biology (Cambridge, UK) discovered the potential of using antibodies in vitro to fight diseases.

1976: The research team of Michael Bishop and Harold Varmus at the University of California, San Francisco, showed that disturbances in one or more members of a family of genes could lead to the transformation of a normal cell into a cancer cell.

1976: Genentech was founded by venture capitalist Robert A. Swanson and biochemist Dr. Herbert W. Boyer.

1981: Genentech scientists John McGrath and Art Levinson cloned and sequenced a portion of the human HER2 gene for the first time.

1984: George Kohler and Cesar Milstein win the Nobel Prize in Medicine "for theories concerning the specificity in development and control of the immune system and the discovery of the principle for production of monoclonal antibodies."

1984: Genentech scientist Axel Ullrich and Peter Seeberg, in collaboration with Mike Waterfield at the Imperial Cancer Research Fund and Joseph Schlesinger at the Weizmann Institute, published the complete human EGF-R sequence in Nature.

1985: Following work that began in the early 1980s, a Genentech team of scientists, including Axel Ullrich and Art Levinson, clone the first full-length human HER2 gene. This achievement is described in a paper published in Science.

1985: Stu Aaronson at the National Institute of Health showed that the HER2/neu gene is frequently amplified in human breast tumors.

1987: Michael Shepard, Axel Ullrich, and their teams at Genentech developed mouse 4D5, the parent of Herceptin, simultaneous with the discovery by Dr.

Dennis Slamon at UCLA and colleagues at the University of Texas Health Science Center, that linked HER2overexpressionn with a more aggressive type of breast cancer found in approximately 25 percent of patients. Further work by Shepard's group demonstrated that the 4D5 could suppress the growth of HER2 over-expressing tumor cells and enhance their sensitivity to killing by the host immune system. Further proof of concept was the demonstration by the Genentech and UCLA teams that radio-labeled 4D5 could localize to HER2-overexpressing tumors in patients.

1989: Michael Bishop and Harold Varmus were awarded the Nobel Prize in Medicine for their discovery that normal cells contain genes capable of becoming cancer genes.

1990: Len Presta, Paul Carter, and Michael Shepard of Genentech create Herceptin by humanizing the 4D5 mouse antibody directed at HER2.

1992: Genentech filed an Investigational New Drug Application (IND) with the U.S. Food and Drug Administration (FDA), and Phase I clinical trials were initiated.

1993: Genentech initiated two Phase II clinical trials that evaluated the investigational anti-HER2 antibody as a single agent and combined it with chemotherapy in the relapsed setting.

1995: Genentech began enrollment of the Phase III pivotal trials for patients with HER2 over-expressing metastatic breast cancer. Genentech worked closely with breast cancer patient advocates to design an expanded access program to ensure the investigational agent is available to patients with no other therapeutic alternatives. Genentech advanced the construction of a new manufacturing facility to produce the anti-HER2 antibody.

1996: Critical efforts are undertaken to enroll patients into the trials. Genentech clinicians and outside investigators spearheaded an amendment to the study protocol of pivotal trial 648 to include paclitaxel chemotherapy as an alternative to doxorubicin chemotherapy. They traveled across the country to inform investigators to spur interest in the trial. Genentech and patient advocates worked together to publicize the tests to the breast cancer community.

March 1996: Researchers at Memorial Sloan Kettering co-authored a paper titled "Phase II Study of Weekly Intravenous Recombinant Humanized Anti-p 185HER2 Monoclonal Antibody in Patients with HER2-Neu-Over-Expressing Metastatic Breast Cancer," which showed that the antibody was clinically active in women with HER2-neu-over expressing metastatic breast cancer who had received prior therapy. The study provided evidence that targeting growth factor receptors caused regression of human cancer cells.

December 1996: Genentech partnered with diagnostic company DAKO to develop a commercial test to identify patients who overexpress the HER2 gene.

March 1997: Genentech completed enrollment of Phase III pivotal trials for the anti-HER2 antibody (now known as Herceptin Trastuzumab).

May 1998: Genentech submitted a biologic license application (BLA) for Herceptin, and DAKO submitted a pre-market approval (PMA) application to the FDA for the diagnostic Herceptin Test. The FDA designated Herceptin as a "Fast Track" product for the treatment of metastatic breast cancer.

May 1998: Results from a Phase III investigational clinical trial of Herceptin were presented at the American Society of Clinical Oncology (ASCO) annual meeting. Results showed that Herceptin, in combination with chemotherapy, increased time to disease progression and response rates.

July 1998: Genentech and Roche signed a licensing agreement giving Roche exclusive marketing rights for Herceptin outside the United States.

September 1998: Herceptin received FDA approval for use in women with metastatic breast cancer who have tumors that overexpress the HER2 protein. It is indicated for treating patients as first-line therapy in combination with paclitaxel chemotherapy and as a single agent for those who have received one or more chemotherapy regimens. Herceptin was the first therapeutic antibody targeted to a specific (HER2) cancer related molecular marker to receive FDA approval.

August 2000: European Commission approved Herceptin to treat HER2-positive metastatic breast cancer.

December 2000: Enrollment of two Phase III clinical trials evaluating the potential use of Herceptin for the adjuvant treatment of early-stage HER2-positive breast cancer was initiated. Adjuvant therapy is given to women with early-stage (localized) breast cancer who have had initial treatment - surgery with or without radiation therapy – intending to reduce the risk of cancer recurrence and the occurrence of metastatic disease. The studies are sponsored by the National Cancer Institute (NCI), part of the National Institutes of Health, and conducted by a network of researchers led by the National Surgical Adjuvant Breast and Bowel Project (NSABP) and the North Central Cancer Treatment Group (NCCTG).

March 2001: Further data from a pivotal Phase III clinical trial were published in the New England Journal of Medicine (NEJM) that showed a significant increase in survival for women with HER2-positive metastatic breast cancer who received Herceptin and chemotherapy over chemotherapy alone.

May 2005: Results from a joint analysis of the Phase III NSABP and NCCTG clinical trials evaluating the addition of Herceptin to standard adjuvant therapy for early-stage HER2-positive breast cancer were presented at the ASCO annual meeting. According to this 3-year planned joint analysis, Herceptin in combination with chemotherapy significantly reduced the risk of cancer recurrence.

February 2006: Based on results from the joint analysis of the NSABP and NCCTG trials, Genentech filed a supplemental Biologics License Application (sBLA) with the FDA for Herceptin for the adjuvant treatment of early-stage HER2-positive breast cancer.

November 2006: The FDA approved Herceptin as part of the treatment regimen containing doxorubicin, cyclophosphamide, and paclitaxel for the adjuvant treatment of patients with early-stage HER2-positive, node-positive breast cancer based on the joint analysis of the NSABP and NCCTG studies.

January 2008: Based on the HERA one-year data, the FDA approved Herceptin as a single agent for the adjuvant treatment of early-stage HER2-positive nod-positive breast cancer or node-negative (ER/PR – negative or with one high-risk feature) following multi-modality, anthracycline-based therapy.

May 2008: FDA approved two new Herceptin-containing regimens for the adjuvant treatment of early-stage HER2-positive node-positive or node-negative (ER/PR-negative or with one high-risk feature) breast cancer.

LIVE W I D E
Reader's Reflections

What is your favorite quote?

What would three things be on your bucket list if you were facing your mortality?

What would your inner circle say about you at a celebration of your life? What music would you have played?

What will you do to LIVE W I D E today?

Go raibh maith agat ~ Thank you ~ Merci ~ Danke ~ Gracias

Talk to a tree.

Start a journal.

Carry a quote book.

Say something quote-worthy.

Walk barefoot someplace you wouldn't dare.

Dance in the shower.

LISTEN TO THE MUSIC SO INTENTLY THAT IT MOVES YOU TO TEARS.

Denounce The Odds.

Buy red tulips. For yourself. Or someone you like.

Slay a Dragon.

Write. Write. Write.

Contemplate the Meaning of Life.

Followed by doing something completely and utterly silly.

REMEMBER: LIFE IS MEANT TO BE *LIVED*.

Live W I D E.

The Trilogy

LIVE WIDE

Original Unpublished Manuscript
St. Patrick's Day, March 17th, 2016

UnBreakable Girl

Pearl Harbor Day, December 7th, 2023*

Unwritten

TBD

Anticipated. Like most things in life, dates are tentative at best.

OH, AND JUST ONE MORE THING...

As the author completed her manuscript and read it cover to cover, she had a disturbing epiphany. The very metaphors she used for her Inflammatory Breast Cancer ... The Dragon, The Awful Possibility, The Demon, Showering with The Enemy, The Pirate Ship...were threats from her childhood. Her subconscious spoke to her through her creative writing, accessing deeply repressed memories.

These traumatic memories surfaced after decades of dormancy, which is not uncommon for survivors of Childhood Sexual Abuse. But the author decided to keep her beak obediently shut and have a nice cup of tea. Or did she?

The second book in the trilogy, Unbreakable Girl, is the one-two punch that reveals her clinically documented history of abuse and the "post-cancer apocalypse" her biological family unleashed. Now the "breadcrumbs" in Live Wide make sense. Her family resorts to unthinkable tactics to destroy her life. Instead of taking accountability or extending an apology. Which is all she asked for.

Unbreakable Girl unearths a groundswell of previously "quiet" research that links Childhood Sexual Abuse (CSA) to a much higher risk of cancer as an adult. Other nasty "after affects" of CSA include eating disorders, PTSD, depression, alcohol abuse ... the list goes on.

One in eight women will be diagnosed with Breast Cancer in her lifetime. One in five will be sexually abused before the age of eighteen.

The second book begins like the first, "Negotiating with The Universe from The Bathroom Floor."

Where most intrafamilial childhood sexual abuse occurs.

Please pass this along to someone who might not be able to afford a hard copy of this book and make their life wider.

Reader's Name: Date:

1. _____

2. _____

3. _____

4. _____

5. _____

6. _____

7. _____

8. _____

9. _____

Merci beau coup ~ Merci beau coup ~ Merci beau coup

www.ingramcontent.com/pod-product-compliance
Lightning Source LLC
Chambersburg PA
CBHW060911120626
46553CB00001B/286